Connecting with the Weather

SPIRITUAL, MAGICAL AND PRACTICAL WAYS OF WORKING WITH WEATHER

HANNAH SEMPLE

GREEN MAGIC

Green Magic
53 Brooks Road
Street
Somerset
BA16 0PP
England
www.greenmagicpublishing.com

Designed and typeset by Carrigboy, Wells, UK
www.carrigboy.co.uk

ISBN 978-1-915580-43-6

GREEN MAGIC

Contents

Acknowledgements

I would like to thank my father for inspiring my love of weather and my mother for encouraging my writing. Both no longer with me, this book is for them.

Thank you also to my partner and children who always support my endeavours and the chaos that sometimes comes with them.

Introduction

As a child, I was captivated by the weather – the way raindrops raced each other down the windowpane, the way the world fell silent after snowfall, and the way the winds whispered in the wheat fields I played in.

As I got a little older, my fascination held, and one year, when on holiday in Devon, my family and I stayed in a cottage where there was seaweed hung by the front door. Curious, I asked my dad about it, and he told me about weather predictions, weather lore, and spoke of something called a barometer. We had a barometer at home, but I had never taken much notice of it until then. It turns out that barometers are pretty awesome.

Now as an adult, I have a barometer of my own; my captivation with the weather has continued but has turned into a deepening relationship. I started connecting with it in more meaningful ways through observation, listening, poetry, and intuition. Through these mediums, weather has become something that grounds me and inspires me, and whether it is magically, spiritually or practically, it is something that I am always connected to.

I hope this book highlights the wonder of connecting with weather and how it can help you gain insight, deepen your spiritual path, and provide you with a greater appreciation of something we experience every day.

CHAPTER ONE

Warm Expectations – Sunshine

The sun shines every day. Some days we barely see it due to cloaks of grey draped across the sky, but it is always there. Sunshine as a weather condition is different from the sun being present every day, and here we shall work with the sun when visibly shining.

Connecting with Sunshine Spiritually and Magically

When working with sunshine, it is important to remember all the seasons, as sunshine connection is different in each season. It is also helpful to know that magically sunshine is connected to the element of fire and can be used for workings in banishing, cleansing, confidence, empowerment, joy, manifestation, purification, rebirth, strength, transformation, and vitality. Sunshine is also connected to air.

Spring

Sunshine varies in spring, but on average there are 400 hours of sunshine during the season, with a daylight average of 13 hours. The sun is not at full strength in this season but grows as the season goes on. Over the course of spring, you will notice that the sun climbs a little higher in the sky each day, which is why spring sunshine is ideal to work with in matters of growth and aspirations.

Aspirations Soul Prompt

You will need:

- Pale yellow paper, cut in the shape of two suns
- Something to write with

On the first day of spring sunshine, take your paper and writing implement out in a quiet spot in nature. Find a location where you can feel the sun's slight warmth upon you and get comfortable in a seated position.

On the first paper sun, write down: *"What are my aspirations for this coming year?"*

Now close your eyes and focus on this question. When you have an answer, write down what it is on the first paper sun.

On the second paper sun, write down: *"What one thing can I do this week towards my aspiration?"*

Again, close your eyes and focus on this thought. When you have an answer, write it down on the second paper sun.

Sit for a while embracing the spring sunshine before heading home. Put the paper suns somewhere you will see them every day and start working on your one step. When you have completed this one step, focus again on what another step could be. You do not have to go out on every occasion, but it may help to recreate the original focus.

Sunshine Growth

Sunflowers are the ideal plant to sow in spring to symbolise both sunshine and growth.

You will need:

- A yellow candle
- A nontoxic writing implement
- A small piece of biodegradable paper
- A sunflower seed
- A small pot filled with soil or compost or a mix

During early April, on a day of sunshine, take your items outside. If you cannot get out, then that's fine – this can be done indoors also.

Light the candle and stare into the flame, whilst pondering on what growth in your life would be beneficial right now. Perhaps it is money, or it could be a positive personality trait, such as patience.

Write whatever it is that you wish to grow on the piece of paper and then bury the paper in the pot.

Take your sunflower seed and sow it into the pot, making sure it is pointy end down at about 2cm in depth. Dampen the soil and say a few words as you do this.

"As the spring sun grows each day, may growth also come my way."

Extinguish your candle and place your pot on a sunny windowsill, planting outside after all chance of frost has gone.

Summer

The sun is at its highest during this season, and there is an average of 600 hours of sunshine during the summer months. While daylight lasts 16 hours, the actual hours of sunshine only average out at six hours per day. The summer sunshine is not all joyful hours of light – sometimes it can be quite heavy and oppressive – but the main theme is strength.

Connecting with the idyllic summer sun is easy, and here are two ways you can try.

Summer's Rest

This can be done in any openly sunny location on a comfortably warm day, whether it is your back garden, the local park, or the beach. Make sure your skin is protected from the sun and that the day is not too hot for you to be able to spend 15 minutes outside.

Now lie down on your back, making sure you are comfortable, and then gently close your eyes. Clear your mind of everything – just let go and focus on your senses of feeling, hearing and scent.

Feel the sun's warmth upon your skin – this is the feeling of summer sunshine days.

Listen to the sounds around you – these are the sounds of summer sunshine days; maybe it is the idle droning of a bee or the waves coming into shore.

Sniff the air around you – these are the scents of summer sunshine days; perhaps you can smell the salty air or freshly cut grass and fragrant flowers.

Most importantly, relax! This is the feeling of summer's rest when otherwise you might be hurtling at top speed.

Dappled Sun

You will need a pen and paper.

On a beautiful day of sunshine, find a quiet glade of trees to sit beneath. If there is a stream or pool there too, then all the better.

Get comfortable, and as you sit, watch how the sunshine dapples through the leaves, how it glints. What colours, feelings and words come to mind? Write them down on your paper.

Sit for as long as you want, taking in everything with your senses. Then, on your return home, try and recapture your experience in a creative form, whether poetry or art.

The other aspect of summer sunshine is those days when it is just too hot. The joy can sometimes be hard to find on days like these when you cannot be bothered to do anything. It is days like these when the power of the sun is really felt, and a good activity is to use the strength of the sun to draw strength to you.

Quick Strength Draw

Step outside. Stand firmly toward the sun with your eyes closed and arms outstretched to the sky. Say:

> "Thank you, Divine, for sunshine days, skies of blue and warming rays.
> I feel your power, your strongest time; may a little of your strength be mine."

Step back inside and cool down.

Autumn

There are still plenty of sunshine days to experience in autumn, with an average of 280 hours for the season. Daylight hours decrease, and the sun's power is starting to wane, yet there is a golden glow at this time of the year, even with the days cooling. It is a time of change and of letting go.

Sunshine Message

Walks on sunny days are a wonderful way to connect with the sunshine all year round, with autumn walks seeming to be particularly poignant. So, on a beautiful sunny autumn day, take a walk.

Notice how the sunshine days look different now that the sun is losing some of its strength. It is a reminder that even things that remain constant in life will change. Notice all the tiny things that the sun's rays touch – the blade of grass, the fading flower, the seed heads of plants. What do you think the sun is saying this season? Note whatever comes to mind and write it down.

Golden Leaves Visualisation

This guided visualisation transcript uses the waning sun and autumn's aspects. Ideally, a recording should be made so you can listen to it later.

> Find a quiet place where you will not be disturbed and sit in a relaxed position with your back straight but not rigid. Gently close your eyes and take a few deep breaths, emptying your mind.
>
> Now, imagine it is an autumn day, the sky is a faded blue, and the sun is shining a golden light upon all below.
>
> (Pause)
>
> In front of you there is a tree; it is an old tree, tall and wide with a beautiful crown of yellow leaves glinting golden in the sunlight.
>
> (Pause)
>
> As you sit, you see a single leaf fall, fluttering through the sky gracefully. It lands gently beside you. You pick it up and notice there are words written on it: "Letting go."
>
> What does this mean to you?
>
> (Pause)
>
> More and more leaves start to fall, dancing merrily before landing on the ground, which shines golden with them. The tree is almost bare now, and the sun seems to blaze a little brighter for a moment as if it is telling you something – letting you know that it is okay to let go.

What is it that you need to release?

(Pause)

You sit among the carpet of golden leaves, feeling the warmth of the autumn sun cocooning your being until the sun starts to cool.

Now gently open your eyes. Have a drink or a nibble on something, and write down everything that came to mind.

Winter

Sunshine days are at their lowest during winter, with an average of 78 hours over the entire season and a daylight sunshine average of 1.5 hours. Much of the winter sky is covered in an impenetrable grey cape. The sun has become meek – not weak or feeble, but resting. Many people will suffer during the winter months due to the lack of sunlight, from feeling a little down to suffering with Seasonal Affective Disorder (S.A.D.). The lack of sunshine, however, is intended to enable us to rest, but bringing some sunshine into the home or embracing the sun are great ways to help us cope better.

Sunshine Walks for Wellness

As the sunshine days are fewer, it is best to make the most of them, as the sun helps to provide us with vitamin D, which can often be lacking in people during the winter. Getting out in the sunshine during winter is also important for your mental health; it breaks up the cycle of lethargy that can occur at this time of year and lessens the impact of depression through increased serotonin levels from the sunshine. Yes, it is cold, so wrap up warm and embrace the sun.

Bringing in the Sun

There are lots of ways that you can bring the sunshine into your home, with the easiest being to make sure as much natural light as possible is coming in through the windows.

Other ways include using the colour yellow to represent the sun in arts & crafts and other activities, having vases of yellow flowers on display, or placing a suncatcher in the window that captures those shining glints of sunlight.

Growing Sunshine

The winter solstice, which occurs each year on the 21st or 22nd of December in the northern hemisphere, is the shortest day of the year. Meaning that daylight hours are at their shortest on this day, but each day after this, the days will slowly get a little longer. Celebrate the growing sun with an activity.

You will need: yellow paper which you will cut into the shape of a sun, and further yellow paper that you will need to cut into about 70 strips.

On day one, which will be the winter solstice, take your sun-shaped yellow paper and attach a loop of string to it so you can hang it up. Say: *"Sun, your power may be low, but each day your strength will grow."*

On day two, take one of your paper strips and loop it to make a circle, secure it with glue or tape and attach it to your paper sun. Say: *"A little more each day, each hour, grow more in strength and more in power."*

Repeat this every day, looping one paper strip through the previous one, repeating the same words from day two, and finishing on the first day of spring.

The same activity could be done with knitting. Start knitting a scarf at the winter solstice, knitting some each day until spring. Not only have you celebrated the strengthening sun, but you have also got a scarf for next winter or a gift for a friend or loved one.

Connecting with Sunshine through Science, History and Lore

Sunshine is electromagnetic radiation emitted by the sun, and it is made up of three distinct types of light rays: visible light, infrared and ultraviolet (UV).

Visible light is the light that is seen; infrared rays are felt as warmth. Ultraviolet light is what causes suntans but also comes with some negative health implications when overexposed to it, such as sunburn, skin aging, skin cancer and eye damage.

Our understanding of the sun has grown hugely over the course of time, which ties in neatly with another aspect of sunshine – and that is time.

Before time was more scientifically measured, the sun was a way of telling whether it was day or night. For diurnal species, including humans, the sun going down was an indicator of sleep, and vice versa for nocturnal animals.

In agricultural communities, the sun's growing and diminishing light was a useful time marker in the sowing and harvesting of plants, and some nomads used these same ideas when following migrating animal herds.

Daily time patterns were measured using the sun by ancient civilisations, with the first known sundial dating back to 1500 BCE in Ancient Egypt. It was created using a rod known as a 'gnomon', which cast shadows on a surface. Modern sundials often feature high-precision engineering using split gnomons for more exact timings, and many are crafted to look aesthetically beautiful.

To connect with sunshine in its more practical aspect of time is to make a sundial. It is a fairly simple activity, and instructions can easily be located online.

The solar year is the generally accepted way today of measuring the yearly cycle, and one of the oldest solar calendars is the Julian calendar, which was proposed in 46 BCE, but today it is the Gregorian calendar that is used in most parts of the world.

Another interesting aspect of the sun is that it dictates the colour of the sky by emitting white visible light, which contains all perceivable colours, and interacting with the atmosphere.

Blue sky seen in the daytime occurs where sunlight hits gas particles in the atmosphere, scattering shorter, smaller light waves of blue and violet in all directions. As the human eye is more sensitive to blue, this is why we see blue skies on sunshine days.

Red/orange skies occur because the sun is lower on the horizon and the light must travel through a thicker layer of atmosphere. Due to this, the shorter light waves of blue and green are scattered away, and the longer light waves of red, yellow and orange are what remain to be perceived.

Weather Lore

One of the most famous weather lore sayings about sunshine involves the colour of the sky, and it says, *"Red sky at night, sailor's delight,"* or alternatively, *"Red sky at night, shepherd's delight,"* which means that a red sunset is an indicator of the following day having fair weather.

This phrase has been in existence for over 2,000 years and more than likely originates from the *New Testament* in Matthew 16:2-3. The adage is accurate to some extent, but this is generally with weather patterns that are at mid-latitude, moving from west to east, such as those in Europe and the US.

Connecting with Sunshine through Nature and Deity

The sun is an important aspect of nature, as it helps to drive the earth's natural systems, such as energy for growth, fuelling the water cycle, and, as we have looked at, dictating the seasons.

One way the sun aids in these systems is through photosynthesis, which is an essential process for plants to produce energy and, in turn, support the entirety of the food chain.

The hydrological cycle is another system that relies on the sun. It is the sun's energy that evaporates the water from the oceans, lakes and soil, causing precipitation (rain) to feed rivers and sustain the environment.

Other weather systems occur due to the sun's uneven heating of the earth's surface.

It is the varying sunlight that creates the seasons and affects plant life cycles and animal hibernation and migration.

Animals and Sunshine

Sunshine does not just affect humans and natural systems; animals need the sun too, in a variety of ways.

Cold-blooded animals such as reptiles, amphibians and fish rely entirely on the sun shining to raise their body temperature.

Sunlight affects the daily behaviours of animals, as well as seasonal behaviours in regulating sleep patterns.

Vitamin D is needed by animals too.

Some animals, like turtles or birds, use the sun to dry out their skin or feathers to kill bacteria or parasites.

Increased sunlight produces serotonin in animals, just like in humans, which helps prevent them from becoming lethargic and depressed.

Humans feel the effect of sunny days when they become too hot, and animals and plants are no different. We can help by making sure plants are well watered to prevent wilting and that our gardens provide places of shade for animals, as well as putting out fresh water for them.

Because the sun is such an important part of earth's cycles and a constant presence worldwide, every culture globally has a sun deity, and many cultures have multiple. Deities such as Ra, Helios, Apollo and Sol are quite well-known, but a lesser-known deity to connect with is Saulė.

Saulė is a solar goddess from Lithuanian and Latvian mythology and is considered one of their most powerful deities – she is responsible for all life on earth. As a matriarch figure, she is the mother of Žemyna, Indraja, Sėlija, Žiezdrė and Vaivora, who are the planets Earth, Jupiter, Saturn, Mars and Mercury, respectively, and she is also considered the patroness of the unfortunate, especially orphans.

Her feast day is celebrated at the midsummer solstice, but this was Christianised, being renamed Saint Jonas' Festival. The winter solstice is acknowledged as Saulės return.

Connecting with Saulė

Celebrate the summer solstice by greeting the sun on the solstice morning and watching it rise.

Make a floral wreath with red and white flowers, which are two colours associated with Saulė.

Build a bonfire.

Learn about the magical fern flower, which is associated with Saulė.

Spend time stargazing. In one of Saulė's stories, she is rescued by the zodiac.

Give to charity.

Create an altar to Saulė, where you could include ribbons, roses, pictures or figurines of white horses, and the colours red, white, gold and silver, which are all associated with her.

Connecting with Sunshine in Other Ways

Have a picnic.

Make suncatchers.

Go on seasonal sunshine walks.

Find music that reminds you of the sunshine and create a sunshine playlist.

Make sunshine-infused water.

Create shadow animals.

Make a fan.

Observe and record sunshine sunny days and temperatures.

Write a sunshine poem or read some sunshine poems.

SUNSHINE

Your tender kisses warm our hearts,
Your gentle touch, it stirs our souls,
Your presence in cerulean skies,
And fiery passion makes us whole.
Basking in your golden glow,
We welcome you with open arms,
Your radiance smiles upon us all,
Through your effervescent charms.

Sunshine is one of the easiest weather conditions to connect with, as most of us are happy to embrace the sun. I hope I have given you some more in-depth ways of connecting with every aspect.

CHAPTER TWO

Umbrella Weather – Rain

Rain is not the most favoured of weather in the UK, and with rain occurring one in three days, it is hardly surprising. Rainy days are usually accompanied by the cold and wind, plus they tend to be dark and gloomy. It is not all negative, however. Rain has some incredibly positive aspects, which we will look at.

Connecting with Rain Spiritually and Magically

Rain is categorised into several types, each with its own characteristics. Here we will look at the basic categories, which I have listed below, and select a few to work with. Rain is connected to the element of water and can be used in magical workings for emotions, cleansing, love, scrying, relationships, intuition and purification. Rain is also connected to the element of air.

Drizzle – very light rain in fine drops.

Shower – a sudden and short outburst of rain.

Sprinkle – a few light drops.

Light rain – gentle soft rain.

Heavy rain – strong pouring rain.

Torrential rain – extremely heavy and intense rain.

Thunderstorm – rain accompanied by thunder and lightning.

Hail – frozen rain.

Appreciating Rain

To begin appreciating rain, it helps to look at its positive aspects. Have you ever noticed how green and vibrant the landscape looks after rainfall? This is known as the 'green effect', and there are a few key reasons why this occurs.

- Rain washes away any dust and debris from the plants' leaves, allowing their green colour to shine through again
- Due to hydration, the plants become perkier
- Rain delivers key nutrients, such as atmospheric nitrogen – a crucial component of chlorophyll, which produces the green colour in plants
- Wet surfaces are reflective, so the landscape becomes increasingly saturated with the colour green more vividly

To experience the green effect and rain itself, an ideal time to go for a walk is when the rain is light. Dress appropriately, bringing with you an umbrella, a magnifying glass and a camera.

As you are walking, take time to appreciate just how green the world is becoming. Start looking for plants that have raindrops on them, and use your magnifying glass to study the raindrop on the leaf or flower. How does it look to you? What feelings are coming to you? Take a close-up photo of the raindrop to look at again later.

Now look at a different plant. Do the raindrops look different? Note any differences, take more photos, and when you get home, make a note of your thoughts. Has the experience of looking deeper helped you to appreciate rain a bit more?

Rain Renewal

The green effect makes the world look almost new again, which is why rain is a great type of weather to work with for renewal.

You will need:

- Chalk and a chalkboard
- A white candle
- Matches or a lighter

On a day when it is raining, light your candle and think about 'you' for a while. What about 'you' could do with renewing? Maybe you need more energy, maybe you need to stop procrastinating, or is it that you need to stop caring what others think about you? Whatever it is, you are now going to draw that version of 'you' on the chalkboard – the 'you' that procrastinates, or has no energy, or worries too much.

After you have finished drawing, extinguish your candle and take your chalkboard out into the rain. Say three times, emphasising the words 'better' and 'today':

> "Rain of renewal, wash away, wash away,
> Renew me for the better, from today, from today."

As it rains, watch the old chalk version of 'you' be washed away, leaving you renewed.

Summer Shower Thankfulness

Rain is not a weather condition we tend to be thankful for, but really, we should be. Rain brings forth life and is much needed at times. An ideal time to say thanks to the rain is during a summer shower on a hot day, when rain brings its coolness.

On a sweltering summer's day, wherever you are, whatever you are doing, when a shower of rain hits, go outside. Raise your head toward the sky, outstretch your arms, and say:

> "Shower of summer rain, who quenches the arid land again,
> And bring relief to all those parched, I thank you now with all my heart."

If you feel like dancing, then I encourage it whole-heartedly.

Heavy Rain Release

"Tears hidden in the rain but not sorrow."

Heavy rain is my go-to in matters of grief, but it can also be worked with for other issues, such as anger, frustration, depression and any instance where you need to release whatever is pent up inside you with a good cry.

Many of us deny tears (which I see as human rain), seeing crying as a sign of weakness. It is not! There are many reasons why crying is beneficial, and I have found that letting the tears flow while out somewhere quiet under an umbrella in the heavy rain is ideal. As nobody else is around, you can just cry, with nature and the rain to soothe you and console your heart.

Here is why crying is good for you:

- It helps to emotionally regulate you, as it activates a part of the nervous system that helps the body relax and detoxifies stress hormones by flushing them out
- Crying helps to ease pain by releasing oxytocin and endogenous opioids
- Due to the release of endorphins, it can help improve mood
- Crying is a critical part of the grieving process, needed to process complex emotions

Torrential Rain

This type of rain is intense, causing flooding, landslides and other disruptions through the power that it yields. This makes it a perfect medium for drawing strength.

In a torrential downpour, take a clean, heavy vessel of some kind and pop it outside to collect the rainwater in. Say:

> "I call upon torrential rain, to fill this vessel to the brim,
> That I may use the relentless power, and all the strength it brings."

After the rain has stopped, take your vessel and decant into a clean jar. I recommend putting it through a sieve or muslin to get rid of any debris. Label the jar and use for magical workings that require strength, such as sprinkling it around the boundaries of your home as a strong protector or watering plants to encourage robust growth.

Connecting with Rain through Science, History and Lore

Rain occurs where atmospheric water vapour has condensed to a point where it is heavy enough to fall. It works in a cyclical way, meaning that the water we have on the planet is all we have, and it is being constantly recycled.

It starts with the sun evaporating water from large bodies of water and landmasses, where it condenses in the atmosphere to form clouds. This condensed water vapour becomes heavy and falls as rain (precipitation), which is then collected by the land and bodies of water.

This cycle is essential for life, with rain benefiting us in many ways, and humans have used it over the course of time in agriculture, gardening, for domestic consumption and as an energy source.

Rain in historical times was extremely important, and in more arid areas where it only occurred at certain times of the year, rain was a matter of survival, with many cultures having rainmaking rituals; in some places, this is still the case today.

Rainmaking

Dodola and Perperuna are two rainmaking customs which were once widespread across southeastern Europe but are today practiced by only a few in remote Albanian regions. The ritual, which takes place in times of drought, includes singing and dancing in a procession that follows a main performer who is dressed in foliage.

Many places in Africa and the Americas also had and still have rainmaking rituals, and it was the Mapuche people of Chile who are recognised as creating the rain stick, which was used to invoke rain.

A simple way to connect with rain would be to make a rain stick. You will need:

- Kitchen towel inner cardboard tube
- Tin foil

- Paper
- Sticky tape
- Rice
- Plus paint, feathers, beads and string for decorating

How to make:

1. Paint the kitchen towel inner tube
2. Place paper over one end and seal it with tape
3. Twist foil into a spiral and place inside the tube
4. Add rice
5. Place paper over the open end and tape it closed
6. Decorate

It is the rice hitting the foil as you move the rain stick that gives it a distinctive sound.

Here in the UK, however, rain is something experienced often, today and historically, so it is easy to see why there are so many historic rain-related words from the different regions.

In Scotland, drizzle was called 'fiss', and 'dibble' was a type of slow rain according to those in Shropshire. In the Welsh Marches, unpredictable seasonal showers were known as 'blunks', and a 'clarty day' was a really wet day in the Lake District.

'Ache and pain' is the Cockney rhyming slang phrase for rain, while some other more specific conditions were 'stoating' from Scotland, where the rain was so heavy it bounced off the ground, and 'plothering', which was heavy rain without wind in the Midlands and North England.

Historically, not only were there many words for rain, but there was much weather lore also, especially when it came to the prediction of rain. A few of the signs to look out for were swallows flying low, leaves showing their underside, drawers and doors becoming sticky and bread becoming soft.

Weather Lore

As for future weather, there are many sayings pertaining to rain, but a general one is: *"A wet March makes a sad harvest."*

First recorded in the mid-19th century, where it appeared in British guides to farming and country living, this weather lore is fairly accurate, especially in the UK. A rainy March often means planting delays, which can reduce harvesting yields. Then there is the damage to soil and sown seeds; rain will wash seeds away, or the soil can become sodden, conditions not ideal for growing.

Connecting with Rain through Nature and Deity

Rain provides essential benefits for nature and the environment. Not only does rain support life, but it also aids in climate regulation and in sustaining ecosystems. Here are a few ways in which it does this:

- Rain replenishes bodies of water, such as rivers, streams, lakes, and the earth's water table, which is essential for those animals that rely on these water sources to survive

- It supports the growth of plants, which is important for ecosystems
- Rain supports habitats, such as rainforests and wetlands, which in turn aids life and biodiversity
- It cools the environment by lowering the earth's temperature
- Rain cleans the atmosphere by washing away pollutants from the air as it falls
- It provides nutrients that are needed for good soil health, which plants need to thrive
- Rain supports the growth of fungi and moss, which at ground level aid in decomposition and returning nutrients to the soil
- Regular rainfall keeps the land moist and less prone to wildfires, keeping habitats and wildlife safer
- Heavier rain aerates the soil through the force with which it hits the ground, breaking up the soil and promoting oxygenation
- Rain supports various species, such as amphibians and insects that rely on water accumulation in the form of ponds and puddles to breed and for general survival

Puddle Jumping

As I previously mentioned, puddles formed from rainfall can be a matter of survival to some creatures, but puddles can also be beneficial to human creatures too. A child will naturally jump in a puddle, but as we get to adulthood, it is something we seem to stop doing, yet it has many health benefits.

Puddle jumping is good for physical fitness as it strengthens muscles while also improving respiratory health. It also supports mental wellbeing by reducing anxiety, boosting mood, and providing a mental time-out, as well as giving us a connection with nature and the weather.

Petrichor

Another aspect of rain in nature we often experience ourselves is petrichor, which is the earthy scent we smell after rain has fallen onto dry soil. The phrase was coined by scientists in 1964 but had been talked of previously in a scientific paper in 1891, yet never scientifically described.

Petrichor occurs due to air escaping from pores in the soil after rainfall to form small bubbles which rise to the surface. On reaching the surface, they release aerosols, which are what carry the scent.

It is believed that the reason humans are able to smell petrichor is due to our ancestors relying on rain more for survival, possibly in the same way camels rely on the smell of it to find water in the desert.

Rain has always been a key element to life since time began. Our ancestors relied upon it, and they were aware of how rain affected the landscapes in which they lived, and there are many rain deities, especially in the hotter regions of the world. An interesting deity to connect with is Mariamman.

Often abbreviated to Amman, she is a Hindu goddess of rain, fertility and healing from the Tamil folk religion and is mostly worshipped in Southern India. Her name means 'Rain Mother', and she is portrayed as a beautiful young woman, usually with two or four arms and red-hued skin.

She is very much still worshipped today, and in the second week of April there is a ten-day festival devoted to her. Bright yellow clothes are worn, and terracotta pots decorated with margosa leaves are carried to her temple.

Connecting with Mariamman

- Make a food offering of pongal, which is a type of rice dish
- Pray to Mariamman for rain during a long dry spell
- Watch fire walking – I am not going to recommend taking part unless you are with an expert (or already an expert yourself)
- Make an outdoor shrine to Mariamman – small villages traditionally have an outdoor shrine made from granite which is associated with her and decorated with lime and red flower garlands
- Wear yellow
- Have a go at making a pot. Terracotta pots are traditionally used to cook the food offering and carry it to the temple
- Create an indoor altar with items placed on there to represent Mariamman, such as a bowl, a trident (which she is pictured as holding), margosa leaves, red flowers, limes and the colour yellow

Other Ways to Connect with Rain

- Singing and dancing in the rain
- Watch raindrops racing down a windowpane
- Create a rain orchestra by placing different objects outside for the rain to hit
- Harvest rainwater to use on the garden in times of dry weather
- Make a rain gauge to observe how much rainfall occurs
- Listen to a rain soundtrack
- Create a playlist of songs that remind you of rain
- Create raindrop art by painting on a piece of paper and allowing the rain to fall on the paper – best done in light rain
- Craft a rain chain from old metal items, chains and string. Examples of rain chains can be found online
- Create your own rain invocation
- Write a poem about the rain or read some rainy poems

SUMMER RAIN

Summer rain
A welcome sound
As tumbling drops
Hit arid ground.
Sweet nature rejoices
In scents of petrichor
And blessed with holy waters
Each plant grows a little more.

Rain might not be the easiest weather to connect with, but it is worth remembering that rain is essential for life to exist, and there are so many positive aspects to it. Sometimes a grey, gloomy, rain-filled day is the weather's way of saying, "Rest a while, and soon you will be renewed."

CHAPTER THREE

Whispers and Shouts – Wind

Wind can be rather a fickle character – not only does it blow in every direction, but it can vary from day to season to location. It can be as calm as a summer breeze or as ferocious as an F4 hurricane, which is why wind is very much associated with change.

Connecting with the Wind Spiritually and Magically

Wind has many aspects that allow for connection and to work magically with, from gentle breezes to full-force gales, although there are limits to working safely with wind, and I would not recommend venturing out into a severe gale where wind speeds reach upwards of 54 miles per hour. Wind is connected to the element of air and is useful in magical workings for cleansing, communication, divination, focus and visualisation.

Working with wind spiritually or magically is dependent on the speed of the wind, which can be measured with the Beaufort Scale. Invented in 1805 by a hydrographer in the Royal Navy named Francis Beaufort, the scale was originally tailored to seafarers. It did not include measured speed, but each type of wind was numbered from zero to twelve and given a description and a visual identification of how the sails of the ship reacted and the sea looked. The scale was modernised for contemporary use, where both land and sea conditions were described, and speeds were included in knots, miles per hour (mph) and kilometres per hour (kph).

THE BEAUFORT SCALE

Number	Description	Speed	Visible Conditions
0	Calm	1 mph	Smoke rises vertically
1	Light Air	1-3 mph	Direction shown by smoke but not strong enough to move a weather vane
2	Light Breeze	4-7 mph	Wind felt on face; leaves rustle
3	Gentle Breeze	8-12 mph	Leaves and small twigs in constant motion; light flags extended
4	Moderate Breeze	13-18 mph	Raises dust and loose paper; small branches moved
5	Fresh Breeze	19-24 mph	Small trees in leaf begin to sway
6	Strong Breeze	25-31 mph	Large branches in motion; whistling heard; umbrellas used with difficulty
7	Near Gale	32-38 mph	Whole trees in motion; inconvenience felt when walking against the wind
8	Gale	39-46 mph	Twigs break off trees; progress impeded
9	Severe Gale	47-54 mph	Slight structural damage (chimney pots and slates removed)
10	Storm	55-63 mph	Seldom experienced inland; trees uprooted
11	Violent Storm	64-72 mph	Very rarely experienced; widespread damage
12	Hurricane	73+ mph	Devastation

On the Beaufort Scale, numbers 6 and 7 come with advisorys, and 8 onwards carry warnings. As a safety precaution, working with any wind that is above a Beaufort rating of 6 is not advisable.

Working with Wind Speeds

Beaufort numbers 0 to 1 – calm to light air. The conditions here are ideal for visualisation and breath focus, as neither of these activities require the sound of the wind but merely the feeling.

Breath focus is the practice of bringing attention to the natural sensations of your breath, just like the natural breath of the air. There are many benefits to breath focus, including calming the nervous system, improving focus, managing anger, and reducing stress and anxiety. The practice of breath focus is outlined below.

1. Find a quiet place and sit in a relaxed upright position, but not with your spine rigid
2. Close your eyes and bring your breath into your awareness
3. Notice the feeling of the air being drawn in and then exhaled through your nostrils
4. If you find your mind drifting, acknowledge it and then bring the focus back to your breath

Those new to breath focus should start with a short session of two to five minutes, as it does take practice, and you should not be disheartened if you seem to struggle with it. A more experienced individual could practice for 10 to 30 minutes, depending on how experienced they are.

Visualisation

This practice is great for connecting with the wind without needing the wind at all, whether as a sensation or sound. This can be done inside, so it is also good for those who struggle to get out.

Start by finding a quiet spot where distractions and disturbances will be unlikely.

Summer Breeze Visualisation Transcript

Different people imagine in several different ways – you may see vivid pictures or imagine words, sounds, feelings, or ideas.

Whichever way you imagine is absolutely fine, so let us begin.

Sit in a comfortable position, keeping your back straight but not rigid. Close your eyes or fix your eyes on one spot (whichever you prefer), softening your gaze.

Settle yourself by taking a few deep, slow breaths. Now imagine you are in a meadow; it is a beautiful warm summer's evening, the grass is long, and the meadow flowers are in bloom.

(Pause)

As you are there, a breeze starts to blow. There is a gentle warmth to it, and you can feel it softly against your skin.

You spot a butterfly with burnished bronze wings being swept along by the changing air flow.

(Pause)

Are you the butterfly accepting the winds of change, or are you fluttering your wings in flight?

(Pause)

Bring your thoughts back to the meadow and notice the way the long grass is rippling, coaxed by the breeze that blows. It is rippling towards you, carrying the heady scent of meadow flowers, carrying a message to you as a whisper in the grass.

(Pause)

Did you hear a message? Whether you did or not, stay in the meadow a while longer; watch the way the breeze moves and feels, and how the butterfly dances with the wind. Inhale the scent of the flowers that waft through the air and listen.

(Pause)

You notice the sun is starting to dip and the breeze is cooler. It is time to say goodbye. Slowly open your eyes and return to the present.

Now ground yourself by sipping some water and eating a snack, then write down anything that came to you through the visualisation.

An extra activity to try here would be to create your own guided visualisation of the wind in different settings or seasons.

Beaufort numbers 2, 3 and 4 – light breeze, gentle breeze, moderate breeze. These conditions are where you can start to hear the wind speak and are an ideal time to go wind walking or leaf listening as a spiritual practice.

Wind Walking

This is a meditative walk focusing on the whispers in the wind and allowing them to guide the thoughts of the walker to bring peace, clarity or answers to problems or questions. As a lone activity, it is advisable to walk in safe environments – and along the edge of a cliff, as beautiful as it is, is not an ideal location.

For a wind walk to be effective, it is best that the wind is not too strong, as the noise becomes too distracting to hear any messages.

Leaf Listening

Walking is not an activity for everyone, so an alternative is what I call leaf listening. It is a remarkably easy activity, and all it requires is to just sit in a quiet place where there are trees. Allow the mind to empty and allow the whispers of the wind to speak through the rustling leaves. It is a terrific way to connect with the wisdom of the wind and very calming.

Beaufort numbers 5 to 6 – fresh breeze and strong breeze. Here we have the ideal conditions for releasing spells and drawing spells. In the instance of releasing, it can be as simple as shouting into the wind something you wish to release and allowing the wind to carry your words away, but here I have included two spells to try – one for releasing and another for drawing.

Letting Go Spell for a Windy Day

You will need:

- A black candle (the colour for banishing)
- Matches or a lighter
- Black nontoxic pen or pencil
- A small piece of biodegradable paper

Light your candle and sit with it a while, visualising what it is that you wish to let go of; it could be a bad habit or a negative attitude. Remember to harm none in the making of your spell.

Write down what it is that you wish to let go of on the paper; it can be one word or a short sentence, nothing too long. After which, extinguish the candle safely, and taking your paper, find a place in nature where the wind is blowing well. High places like hills are ideal but not necessary, so long as there is a good wind.

Now take your paper, tear it into tiny pieces, and release them to the wind. As you watch them get carried away, visualise what you wanted to release being gone. If you wish to say a few words as you throw your paper, keep it simple.

"Power of Wind, hear my plea, release what I wish, clear from me."

Stay and feel the wind for a while before heading home.

Kite Drawing Spell

For this you will need a kite. It does not have to be a fancy or expensive one; it can be as simple as paper on string, and there are plenty of tutorials online demonstrating how to make a simple kite.

Think of something you would like to draw to you, and write or draw on the kite words and symbols to represent it, visualising that you already have this thing you wish for. For example, if you wanted to draw happiness, then smiley faces would be a good representation.

Now take the finished kite out on a windy day and fly it as high as you can for at least ten minutes. As it flies, watch the way it moves through the sky, and if you wish to say some words, keep it short, either saying it aloud or in your head.

"Winds of change, draw to me, that which brings positivity!"

Whether you used words or not, after ten minutes bring the kite back in, visualising positive change becoming stronger as the kite draws nearer to you.

Connecting with the Wind through Science, History and Lore

Historically, wind was most important for sailors. In the days when ships had sails, they relied on the power of the wind to propel them forward, so it is hardly surprising that many superstitions about the wind came into being around this time.

Whistling was thought to bring a wind into being, but it had to be done softly; too loud and a storm may well be whistled up, and that was something a sailor definitely did not want.

Scratching the mast with a coin or throwing a coin in the sea was also thought to produce a productive breeze, and sometimes sailors would even buy 'wind knots', which were spells magically created by witches.

Wind knots were pieces of string that had three knots in them, which sailors could use to promote wind by untying the knots. Untying the first knot would cause a breeze to spring up; the second knot would bring a gale. If the third knot were loosened, however, it would unleash a hurricane. I don't expect sailors ever untied the third knot.

Winds are still just as important to seafarers today; they may be less superstitious in modern times, but knowing and reading the wind is crucial, as the wind directly affects the conditions at sea and the progress of sea travel.

There are many types of wind that are helpful for a seafarer to be aware of.

Planetary or Prevailing Winds – These are large-scale winds that are driven by the earth's rotation, and these types of winds include the trade winds, which are probably the most well-known, and they blow from subtropical high-pressure zones towards the equator. They are so named because they were used by sailing ships that were trading goods from Europe to the Americas and Asia. Other prevailing winds are the Westerlies, which flow from west to east at mid-range latitudes, and the Polar Easterlies, which are cold winds blowing eastward from the poles.

Periodic Winds – These are winds that change seasonally or even daily due to variations in temperature. These include monsoon winds, which are seasonal winds that occur in the primary regions of South and East Asia, Northern Australia, Africa, and parts of the Americas. Other periodic winds are the sea and land breezes, which are coastal winds that travel from sea to land during the day and vice versa at night.

It is not just seafarers who rely on the wind or need knowledge of it; mountaineers, for example, need knowledge of winds when climbing, as a safety measure. Historically, millers using windmills would have relied on wind-power to mill the flour. Our wind farms of today rely on wind energy to help power the grid.

Weather Lore

Because of people's reliance on wind, there are many sayings in weather lore about it, and one I have come across states:

> "The west wind always brings wet weather,
> The east wind wet and cold together.
> The south wind surely brings no rain,
> The north wind blows it back again."

Surprisingly, wind weather lore is quite accurate in many ways, although not completely. While a south wind will bring the warmer weather, not always will it be dry, and the east wind certainly does bring the cold, but the wet might not always mean rain but sometimes snow.

Some may remember the 'Beast from the East' in 2018, when the United Kingdom experienced a cold wave with temperatures recorded as low as -14.2°C and snowfall of 22 inches in some places. It certainly gave validity to the weather lore that states:

> "When the winds come from the east, it's neither good for man nor beast."

Connecting with Wind through Nature and Deity

The wind isn't just something that humans have harnessed for practical uses or rely upon. In nature, wind is an influential factor in the environment; it is wind that assists in stripping trees bare ready for winter, but there are many other ways in which the wind works in the natural world.

- Plants rely on wind for pollination
- Fungi rely on wind for spore dispersal
- Wind helps to shape the landscape
- Globally, wind distributes heat and moisture
- Wind clears the air of pollution
- Gentle breezes can help a plant's growth by making it stronger
- Birds use wind currents to conserve energy
- As wind dries plants, this helps to prevent mildew and disease
- Some migrating insects use winds within the jet stream to enable faster travel

We can connect with wind through nature, not just by listening to the leaves in the wind, but also by observing the way the wind affects nature in other ways, such as watching the ripples on water caused by the wind. We can also connect through flowers that have a connection to the wind.

Dandelion clocks are an excellent choice here, as their downy seeds are dispersed by the wind, and a simple activity is to make a wish and blow the clock, watching as the tiny seeds are carried away by the wind.

The ancients knew the importance of wind, and this is represented in the deities that they worshipped. There were wind gods in many cultures, and their worship can be found all round the globe in Europe, Africa, Asia, Oceania, and the Americas.

The Ancient Egyptians had a fair few wind deities, including one for each direction, as too did the Ancient Greeks, where they were collectively known as the Anemoi. Boreas was the god of the north wind, Eurus the god of the east wind, Notus the god of the south wind, and Zephyrus was the god of the west wind.

The Ancient Greeks also had Aeolus, who was the keeper of the winds, and Aura, whose name means 'breeze', who was the goddess of the breeze. Aura's story is not a happy one, but it serves as a reminder as to why revenge, hatred, suspicion and murder are not good qualities to have.

An ideal deity to connect with, however, is Vayu, also known as Pavana, and he is the Hindu god of the winds, as well as the divine messenger of the gods. He is an important deity and is not just seen as a figure but as the essential life force (Prana) that sustains all beings. He controls the respiratory system and is fundamental in yogic practice as the 'breath of life'.

In Ayurveda, Vayu is the element of air, and an imbalance of Vayu, often denoted by indigestion and nervous restlessness, would be treated by balancing the Vata Dosha with relaxation, routine, and warm nourishing foods.

In modern times, Vayu is increasingly being seen as a symbol of clean air where environments face pollution.

Connecting with Vayu

An altar could be dedicated to Vayu with the inclusion of items such as a fan, a white flag, or a gazelle; these are all items Vayu is depicted with. The colour blue is a good incorporation, as Vayu is described as having blue skin.

Kite festivals are held in some places in India to honour Vayu, so flying a kite would be an enjoyable way of connecting whilst at the same time celebrating the power of the wind.

A daily offering to Vayu could include purifying the air in the house by opening all the windows.

As Vayu has become more symbolic of clean air, focusing on environmental work to clean up air pollution is ideal.

With Vayu as the breath of life, practicing yoga or balancing your Vayu through Ayurveda might be something to try.

Connecting with Wind in Other Ways

- Go sailing
- Go windsurfing
- Record the wind using a weather vane
- Observe the wind in different environments, such as by the sea or in the city, and record the differences
- Read or research about the wind
- Write a poem about the wind
- Create something artistic to represent the wind
- Make pinwheels, wind chimes, or a windsock
- Wind dance – dance and mimic the winds movement

- Find and listen to music that reminds you of the wind; create a playlist
- Go hill walking, just to feel the wind

Wind is a wonderful weather to work and connect with, especially if you are wanting change for the better, guidance, clarity, peace, or emotional and physical support.

"The wisdom in the wind whispers to the soul."

CHAPTER FOUR

Look to the Skies – Rainbows and Clouds

Let's start with the sky – the view upward from the surface of the earth that technically includes the atmosphere and outer space but generally refers to the expanse that can be seen with the human eye. Look to the sky, and you will see more than the vast endlessness that can make one feel small and insignificant; you will see the wisp of a cloud or the perfect arc of a rainbow.

Connecting with the Rainbows Spiritually and Magically

A rainbow is an optical weather phenomenon caused by refraction, internal reflection, and the dispersal of light in water droplets. A specific set of conditions is needed for a rainbow to form, which is why working with rainbows can be tricky, as they do not tend to last long; although this is a good reminder that challenges are temporary. Rainbows are connected to the elements of air, water, and fire, as all three are required for a rainbow to occur. Magically, you can work with a rainbow for any of the associations connected to these three elements. Refer to chapter eight for a list.

Rainbow Troubles

On seeing a rainbow in the sky, get outside if possible, and while you look at it, think about any troubles you are currently having before saying:

> "Red and yellow, orange, and green, indigo, blue, and violet beams,
> I ask your colours of every shade, to take my troubles as you fade."

Rainbow Communication

To connect with rainbows without seeing one, you can use the rainbow colours in a working for communication – often in myth rainbows are seen as bridges between two worlds.

You will need a piece of blank paper and pens to represent each colour of the rainbow, plus a black pen.

Is there a part of your life where being able to communicate better would be helpful?

Think about this while on the left side of a piece of paper you draw something to represent yourself in black pen. You do not need to be an artist; a stick man is fine.

Now use the red pen to draw an arc going from yourself to the right side of the paper; as you draw the red, say:

"Red, give me the strength to communicate."

Now take your orange pen and draw an arc beneath the red one, this time saying:

"Orange, give me the warmth to convey openly."

Repeat with each colour, using the words below for each colour:

"Yellow, give me the confidence to speak aloud."

"Green, give me a balanced view."

"Blue, give me the intelligence to understand others."

"Indigo, give me the intuition of knowing."

"Violet, give me the wisdom of words."

Then say:

"Rainbow colours, help me to talk my truth for the betterment of all."

Now place the paper somewhere accessible for when you need to refer to it.

Rainbow Guidance

A rainbow is made of many colours across the spectrum, but we see the seven main colours of red, orange, yellow, green, blue, indigo, and violet. Magically, the number seven is associated with spirituality and guidance – making a rainbow the perfect medium to ask for guidance. Next time you see a rainbow, ask for guidance; maybe it will point you in the right direction.

Connecting with Clouds Spiritually and Magically

Clouds are one of the most visible wonders in our skies. They are made up of tiny water droplets suspended in the air and vary in shape, size, and texture. Clouds are classified into several types according to these factors.

The easiest way to connect with clouds is by simply taking the time to watch them. On a fine sunny day, where white clouds are scudding across the skies, lie down somewhere, whether in the garden, at the beach, or at a local park, and just watch how they move, how they change shape. I always imagine the sky to be like the sea, a great expanse of blue where the clouds are the foamy crested waves. Clouds are connected to the elements of air and water, and magical workings can cover either of the elemental associations.

Grey Day Mindfulness

Sometimes clouds feel oppressive, especially when grey cloud cover blankets the skies, but it does not need to feel like this. These cloud-cloaked skies are an invitation to be still.

Sit quietly beneath these steely skies, just sit. Look at the grey expanse, notice the temperature, whether there is a breeze, what nature is doing, watch the birds in the leaden skies; look for the tiny things that perhaps you would not normally notice.

Life is beautiful, even on grey days.

Cloud Messages

To go deeper with cloud connection, ask the clouds for a message.

On a fine day with plenty of clouds and a gentle breeze, go outside, lie down, look at the clouds, and say:

> "Spirit of clouds, hear my plea, help open my eyes so I may see.
> And as you travel across the skies, impart your message before my eyes."

Some factors to consider when receiving your message include the higher the cloud, the less urgent the message, and slower clouds are telling you of something further into the future. Look at the shapes of the clouds; what comes to mind? Do not agonise over finding something for the cloud to look like; go with what pops into your head or grabs your intuition.

If you do not see anything, that is fine – not all clouds carry messages. After 20 minutes, if no message has come, then try another day. Any message you did receive, look further into – for example, if you saw an elephant, the cloud message may have been prompting you to remember something.

Connecting with the Rainbows through Science, History and Lore

Rainbows have fascinated scientists for centuries, and it was the Greek scholar Aristotle (384–322 BCE) who first paid serious attention to the rainbow and whose explanation for them was unmatched for hundreds of years. In 65 CE, the Roman philosopher Seneca the Younger discussed various theories about the formation of rainbows, and over the decades many other scientists made their own studies and developed their own theories. It was not until the turn of the 14th century that Theodoric of Freiberg provided an accurate geometrical analysis of the rainbow.

It was not just scientists who were fascinated by the rainbow; it has been a part of religion and history since ancient times. Abrahamic religions see the rainbow as being a covenant between God and man, while many other faith groups see it as a bridge of some kind, including the Norse, the Navajo tradition, and Māori mythology, and it is possibly the inspiration for the Floating Bridge of Heaven in Japanese myth.

The rainbow was not always seen as positive, and in Latvian legends it was forbidden to approach a water source if there was a rainbow for risk of being swallowed by the rainbow and then later coming down in the rainfall as bones.

There are many different forms a rainbow can take, including a double or triple rainbow, a twin rainbow, a full circle, and a monochrome rainbow. The double rainbow is where a secondary rainbow, which is fainter in colour, is seen at a greater angle to the primary one, due to a double reflection of sunlight in the raindrops occurring. The dark sky that lies between the two bows is called 'Alexander's Band', named after Alexander of Aphrodisias, who first described it.

Rainbows do not just appear in the daytime or when it is raining; they are visible during other times and conditions also. Monochrome rainbows, which are exceedingly rare, occur when there is a shower at sunset or sunrise and the light becomes scattered, resulting in a dramatic red rainbow. Moonbows, or lunar rainbows, are caused by the light from the moon reflecting in the same way that the sun does during the day.

Rainbows also occur in fog (known as fogbows) and in sleet (known as sleetbows), as water is present in both fog and sleet.

Weather Lore

Weather lore covers predictions according to the time a rainbow is seen, and some even includes descriptions of how vibrant certain colours show. Here we will look at a well-known weather lore saying:

"Rainbow afternoon, good weather coming soon."

This lore is scientifically supported when presented at mid-latitudes, due to weather systems generally travelling from west to east. An afternoon rainbow, therefore, shows rain going eastwards, because the sun is shining from the west.

Connecting with Clouds through Science, History and Lore

It was Aristotle in around 340 BCE who wrote *Meteorologica*, which delved into the knowledge known at the time about natural science, weather, and climate and is where clouds are mentioned. However, the first significant studies did not take place until the beginning of the 19th century. These were done by Jean-Baptiste Lamarck and Luke Howard, with the latter formally classifying the cloud types.

There are many more cloud classifications today, and in 2017, the Cloud Appreciation Society was credited with adding the *asperitas* classification of cloud to the *International Cloud Atlas*.

The main cloud types are separated into three divisions according to their height, known as low clouds, middle clouds, and high clouds.

Low clouds – cumulus, cumulonimbus, stratus and stratocumulus.

Middle clouds – altostratus, nimbostratus and altocumulus.

High clouds include cirrus, cirrostratus and cirrocumulus.

There are also other cloud types, which is where *asperitas* is categorised.

Clouds are often thought of as being white, grey, or black, but other colours are represented in clouds, and this is due to the scattering of light in the atmosphere, where the cloud will take on the colour of the sky. Red, orange, and pink clouds occur almost exclusively at sunset or sunrise. Clouds with a greenish or bluish hue hold substantial amounts of water, meaning a possibility of rain. Yellow clouds are usually due to the presence of pollution or smoke and tend to be seen from late spring to early autumn in regions where forest fires occur and occasionally in urban environments where pollution is at elevated levels.

Coloured clouds feature in Chinese art and are known as *quinyun* or *wuseyun*, meaning 'five-coloured cloud'; it is one of their most auspicious cloud motifs, as it symbolises peace. Clouds have been represented in art since the Shang Dynasty, and clouds have been used by artists over the centuries, incorporating different approaches to serve as a symbol to convey atmosphere, from dark and moody to dynamic or ethereal.

Cloud Art

Look at a variety of artworks with clouds. What do these cloudscapes say to you? How do they make you feel? If you were a cloudscape, how do you imagine your picture would look?

Weather Lore

When it comes to predicting weather through clouds, there are a few sayings, but one of the most well-known states:

> "Mackerel sky, mackerel sky, never long wet, never long dry."

A mackerel sky is a rippling cloud formation of cirrocumulus or altocumulus clouds that resembles the scales of a fish and is a reliable indicator of a shift in weather conditions. Looking at the thickness of the clouds in a mackerel sky allows one to see which way the shift is heading.

Connecting with the Rainbows through Nature and Deity

Apart from in the skies, rainbows also appear in nature where water is present, in waterfalls, mist and sea spray, and while rainbows do not directly help nature, they are a valuable symbol for beauty, peace, and appreciation and conservation of the natural world. They can, however, be seen as an indicator of the presence of clean and clear water, and seeing a rainbow has been shown to have a therapeutic effect, lifting mood and bringing a sense of peace to the viewer.

Many ancient cultures had deities connected to rainbows, including the Mesopotamians, the Aboriginals, and the Mesoamericans. Perhaps the most well-known deity of the rainbow is the Greek goddess, Iris. She is a messenger goddess and seems to have no unique mythology of her own, although there are a few traces of worship on the island of Delos.

She was pictured as a young woman with wings, carrying a caduceus and a pitcher of water. In some depictions, she is seen wearing a coat of many colours, which created the rainbow as she travelled across the sky with her messages, and her wings were said to be able to light up a dark cavern.

Primarily she is associated with communication but is also believed to have aided in fulfilling the prayers of humans, whether by herself or by relaying the prayers to the appropriate deity.

In ancient times, she was considered a lesser goddess with no temples, shrines or sanctuaries known to her, but in a work written by Athenaeus, an Ancient Greek scholar, it is mentioned that the people of Delos did make offerings of a type of cheesecake to Iris.

Connecting with Iris

- Create an altar dedicated to her with rainbow colours, winged creatures, a pitcher of water and a candle to represent her light

- Craft some rainbow-coloured prayer beads
- Pray to Iris
- Write an old-fashioned letter to somebody and send it off
- Send an email or message
- Make a cheesecake in honour of Iris
- Plant the flower iris in your garden

Connecting with Clouds through Nature and Deity

- Clouds are essential to nature, not least of all for precipitation, which replenishes the freshwater bodies around the planet, but in many other ways which are vital
- Clouds reflect approximately 20% of incoming solar radiation back into space, which provides coolness in hot conditions
- They play a role in cleaning the atmosphere by transporting dust and bacteria particles
- Clouds aid atmospheric circulation by taking energy from the warmth of the equator to the poles
- They trap heat which prevents extreme cooling at night
- Clouds provide shade

As much as clouds are important to nature, there are very few deities associated with clouds alone. There are many sky deities that include clouds alongside other aspects such as storms, rain, or lightning, but only two lesser goddesses that rule the clouds: Nephele from Greek and Roman mythology and Sanja from the Hindu faith.

Nephele was created by Zeus, sculpted from a cloud in the image of Hera to trick Ixion, who had tried to assault Hera herself. Ixion, seeing Nephele and thinking it was Hera, did assault her, enraging Zeus and impregnating Nephele. As a creation of an immortal, the making of Nephele could not be undone, and thereafter she became a lesser goddess, giving birth to Centaurus who became the father of the Centaur race, who were half-man and half-horse.

Sanja is the consort of the sun god Surya in the Hindu faith and the goddess of clouds. She represents the cooling, calming influence against his intense heat. At first, she was unable to endure the burning energy of her husband, so she created a shadow version of herself to take her place in the household while she retreated to the forest. Sanja's deception was uncovered, and her father diminished the heat of Surya somewhat to allow Sanja to live with her husband.

Connecting with Nephele and Sanja

Both of these minor goddesses may have been deities of the clouds, but they seem to have many associations with the human conditions of light and dark. If you look at some clouds, you will notice that they are bright white on top and dark underneath, so perhaps these two deities were perfect as cloud goddesses after all.

Dark and Light Clouds

You will need a piece of paper and light- and dark-coloured pens.

On a piece of paper, draw two large clouds big enough to write a list in. Colour the border of one in a light colour and the other in a dark colour. The light cloud will represent your light side and the dark cloud your shadow side.

In the light cloud, write all your positive aspects, and in the dark cloud, all your negative traits. Look at the balance or imbalance between both. Of your negative traits, which one do you think you could work on? Highlight it, work on it and keep your paper safe to review at a later date.

Connecting with the Rainbows in Other Ways

- Utilise colour more in your life through clothing and accessories
- Plant a rainbow garden
- Write or read a poem about a rainbow
- Make a rainbow-catcher with crystals for the window
- Have a rainbow feast
- Create a rainbow sand bottle to represent peace

Connecting with Clouds in Other Ways

- Photograph clouds
- Learn to recognise the different types of clouds
- Do a 'cloud in a jar' experiment
- Find songs that remind you of clouds; create a cloud playlist
- Write or read a poem about clouds

Mayhem and Mystery – Storms and Fog

Storms

A storm is any disturbed state of the natural environment or atmosphere that is significantly different from normal conditions. There is more than one type of storm which affects the entire globe, but we shall work with the type of storms we get here in the UK.

Connecting with Storms Spiritually and Magically

Storms in Britain tend to bring torrential rainfall, thunder, lightning, and high winds. The coastal places get battered by tumultuous seas; flooding can occur, and damage to infrastructure and nature can be devastating. It is not advisable to go out in a full-scale storm, but take extra care if you do. Storms vary in their elemental connections, so it's worth looking at the mechanism of a storm to decipher which elements; for example, a thunderstorm is connected to the elements of water, air, and fire, whereas a coastal storm is connected to just water and air, and a dust storm would be earth and air.

Coastal Storms

Coastal storms are where waves driven by the wind (known as wind waves) and/or storm surges strike coastal regions. The waves hitting the coast will often exceed five metres high. To work with a coastal storm, take precautions.

Storm Release

To release negative emotions, you can scream into a coastal storm; make sure you are far enough away from the waves' reach but can still hear the roar of the storm. Scream out your negative emotions and let the noise of the storm take them from you. Alternatively, you could say: *"Storm spirit, take from me, all my negativity."*

If you would rather stay indoors, here is a visualisation to work with instead.

Get comfortable in a quiet place, in a seated position with your back straight but not rigid. Are you comfortable?

When you are, close your eyes gently or focus on one object.

(Pause)

Take a few deep breaths and let us begin. You are on an island; it is a small island with craggy rocks surrounding it. It is quite bleak and barren.

(Pause)

The skies have become steely grey with oppressive dark clouds, and the wind is stirring, stronger with each moment, shrieking into the leaden sky.

(Pause)

The sea is beginning to get restless, its crested waves heaving, getting ready to release its fury. Rising up, the waves throw themselves onto the dark jagged rocks, water spraying in angry jets.

(Pause)

The tumultuous mass of the brooding sea rises again, a body of negativity and torment, its waves plundering the shore, roaring as each wave crashes, purging itself.

(Pause)

You are that stormy sea, negative emotions welling inside you, needing a release. What negativity can you feel rising beneath the surface of your sea?

(Pause)

Now, as that stormy sea, take all those negative thoughts and amass a great wave and hold it at its brink. Now release; let the wave rush to the coast to crash against the rocks, showering your negativity into droplets that get whipped away by the howling wind.

(Pause)

Repeat the process if you feel it necessary, and when finished, open your eyes or bring your focus back. Have a drink or nibble on something and write down any thoughts.

Thunderstorms

Thunderstorms develop when the atmosphere is unstable and where warm air exists underneath much colder air. They can occur at any time of the year but tend to be more severe in the summer months, usually after a few hot, sticky days of weather.

Thunder is the sound produced by the fast heating of the air caused by a lightning strike, and lightning is an electrical discharge that occurs when there is a negative charge buildup in a cloud and the electrons gravitate towards the positive atoms. Thunderstorms are both negative and positive energies, but like the electrons, I gravitate toward the positive aspects.

Imbue the Positive

When there is a thunderstorm, place magical items that you wish to charge with positivity on a windowsill, or you could place a bowl of water outside to be charged by the storm to use in workings that require a positive boost.

Lightning Insight

You will need paper and something to write with.

One way lightning can be interpreted is as a divine spark, an illumination of the mind, and an activity to try is to use lightning to gain some kind of insight.

Sit quietly and allow your mind to empty. Then at each flash of lightning, write the first thing that comes to mind – don't think, just intuitively write, no matter how silly it might seem.

It does not matter how many lightning strikes there are, whether two or ten, but when the storm is over, read what you have written down. Does it make any sense? If yes, then that's great; if not, keep the paper and review it in a week.

Fog

Fog can be considered as a low-lying cloud, as it is made up of tiny water droplets that are suspended in the air. Fog, though, unlike clouds, stays close to the earth's surface. Mist is similar to fog but more transparent.

Connecting with Fog Spiritually and Magically

Working with fog is to accept the hidden or the unknown. It is a liminal weather, and standing in the fog can be slightly disconcerting, causing confusion and doubt as to which way to go. This is why it is ideal as a medium for meditation in matters of releasing or transitioning, but it can also be used in other ways.

Fog is connected to the elements of air and water, so magical workings using the associations of these two elements are ideal.

Fog Charging

On a foggy day, look at the expanse of fog in front of you, and then charge it with a specific emotion by projecting the emotion visually into it. It must be a positive emotion that you need more of, such as joy or love. Say:

> "I charge this fog, my intention true, to strengthen my emotions as I walk through."

Walk into the fog, repeating the words. Spend a little time in the fog before navigating your way out carefully.

Fog Protection

You will need a smudge stick or joss stick and a lighter.

Light your smudge stick or joss stick. Now look at the smoke coming from it and imagine that this is a swirling fog, a fog of protection and peace. Walk around your home with your stick, visualising that the fog is weaving throughout your home, and say:

> "Spirit of fog in your grey disguise, protect my home from ill,
> May peace prevail within these walls, under your protective will."

When you have been in every part of your home, put out your stick safely.

Connecting with Storms through Science, History and Lore

The word 'storm' comes from the Proto-Germanic *sturmaz*, meaning 'noise' or 'tumult'. Storms are created when a centre of low pressure develops with a system of high pressure surrounding it.

They have been part of our planet's history since time began. Storms appear in the *Epic of Gilgamesh* and *the Bible* and have featured throughout history, impacting human society. There are many distinct types of storm, and I have included a few here to show how different they are.

Blizzard – heavy snow, gale-force winds and frigid conditions.

Dust storm – strong winds that pick up significant quantities of soil or sand, reducing visibility.

Firestorm – created during large bushfires, where the fire is so intense that it sustains its own wind system.

Hailstorm – where the hailstones are greater than 5cm in diameter.

Ice storm – one of the most dangerous winter storms, where all is covered in ice and any rainfall freezes instantly.

It is thought that modern storms have increased in intensity due to ocean temperatures becoming warmer and that, due to storms' slower movement, they cause more damage.

There have been many devastating storms marked in British history since weather records began, and here below are some of the worst ones.

1607 – The Bristol Channel Floods were caused by a storm surge, drowning 2,000 people.

1703 – The Great Storm of 1703 raged for a week, killing thousands of people and sweeping a lighthouse into the sea.

1881 – The Eyemouth Disaster, a windstorm that left 189 fishermen dead, most of them being from Eyemouth in Scotland.

1891 – The Great Blizzard cut Devon and Cornwall off for four days, and 200 people perished.

1953 – The Great North Sea Flood saw 30,000 people evacuated and the death of 326.

1987 – The Great Storm was notoriously dismissed by weather forecasters but left 18 people dead and caused immense damage.

2000 – The floods of 2000 caused major flooding and damage.

2013 – The storms of 2013 saw thousands evacuated and caused widespread damage.

2018 – The Beast from the East sent polar continental air masses to the UK, bringing cold, snow and ice.

Storms, as we seen, have a devastating effect on the lives of humans, and it is always good to remember the power and might of weather, which is the reason that the UK Met Office in 2015 started naming winter storms to improve safety communications.

While it is easy to see the negative side of storms, they have brought positive change; our technology and our systems for predicting and dealing with storms have improved, keeping people safer.

Take a look at your own life. When has something negative brought about positive change?

Weather Lore

Storm weather lore is varied and not as reliable today as it was in the past. One saying states:

"When seagulls fly to land, a storm is at hand."

While this is certainly true, it is less of an indicator due to the numbers of urban gulls living inland today.

Another saying says:

"When the forest murmurs and the mountain roars, then close your windows and shut your doors."

This is a classic and beautiful adage pertaining to the natural elements getting noisy when a storm is coming but is less obvious today due to most people living in more urban environments.

One storm weather lore saying that still stands well is:

> "When the ditch and pond offend the nose, then look for rain and stormy blows."

Scientifically, as a storm approaches, the humidity increases, and the water molecules in the air attach themselves to the odour molecules, which become more intense and appealing to the human nose.

With all our technology, storm predictions are still a bit hit and miss. Take these weather lore sayings and test them out. Let me know how reliable they are for you at: earthmotherauthor@gmail.com

Connecting with Fog through Science, History and Lore

Fog forms when the difference between air temperature and dew point is less than 2.5°C, and water condenses into water droplets that hang in the air. Not unlike stratus clouds, fog occurs when a cool, stable air mass is trapped beneath a warm air mass. Fog produces precipitation in the form of drizzle and sometimes light snow.

Fog causes many interesting effects when we consider that the senses and shadows are cast through fog in three dimensions, which is why the shadows can end up eerie and spectral-looking. Sound also behaves differently through fog. High pitches which operate on a short wavelength become dissipated through fog, but low-pitched notes which work on a long frequency are less affected, which is why foghorns use a low-pitched tone.

There are many types of fog, and historically fog has had plenty of impact on humanity. It was used in warfare to confuse enemies or to escape the enemy, as Washington did in the Battle of Long Island in 1776. One type of fog that has had a significant impact on society is smog.

In December 1952, during a particularly chilly winter, a fog formed over London, which was not unusual for the city. However, due to the cold temperatures, residents of the city were burning more coal on their fires than usual, and the pollutants from the smoke became trapped in the water droplets in the fog, turning it into smog and making it toxic.

The smog lifted after four days, but a heavy price was paid by the people. Approximately 4,000 people died as a result of the toxic smog, and many more were left with breathing problems. Due to this, the Clean Air Acts of 1956 and 1968 were brought into law, and now, because of these laws and modern developments, here in the UK, fog has become a natural weather state once more that can be appreciated.

Weather Lore

Few weather lore sayings about fog exist in the UK, but there is one that says:

> *"A fog in summer is followed by heat"* – and this is often correct.

This is because the conditions needed to create fog (clear skies, calm winds, and high humidity) allow for rapid heating when the sun rises, leading therefore to sunny, warm weather.

Connecting with Storms through Nature and Deity

Storms affect nature in a multitude of ways, depending on what type of storm it is, with negative and positive effects. Negatively, storms cause damage to the environment by uprooting trees, eroding coastlines, flooding, destroying farmland and even causing death. But for every negative aspect, there is a positive.

- Storms are crucial for replenishing water in lakes, rivers, and aquifers; in some regions, storms account for 50% of water replenishment
- Lightning maintains the balance of nitrogen in the soil, benefitting the plants
- Thunder helps to clear the atmosphere
- Storms cool the atmosphere
- Although storms cause erosion, they also redistribute sediment, which rejuvenates coastal areas
- Storms weed out weak and diseased trees, allowing for other vegetation to thrive

In ancient times, there were many storm deities across differing cultures, and several of them were associated with thunder and lightning, among other aspects. The

Etruscans saw lightning as being a sign and developed an extraordinarily complex practice for interpreting lightning strikes. This form of divination is known as 'ceraunoscopy' or 'brontoscopy'.

Perhaps the most well-known storm deities are Zeus, chief deity of the Greek pantheon, and Thor from Germanic Paganism, but another, who is often compared to the previous two, is Perun, the supreme deity of the Slavic pantheon. He is often depicted as a warrior wielding a hammer or an axe, and he reigns over the sky, thunder, storms, lightning, rain, fertility and upholding the law. His associations are the number nine, Thursday, the oak tree, tin, the colour red, the eagle, fire and the iris flower.

Shrines to Perun are found in oak groves and atop of mountains, and his feast day, Perunov Den, is celebrated on August 2nd in the modern calendar and July 20th in the old calendar.

Connecting with Perun

- Create an altar to Perun decorated with his associations
- Plant an acorn
- Celebrate his feast day by having a fire
- Create a display of irises
- Uphold the law
- Build a shrine to Perun or dedicate a local oak tree to him
- Practice storm magic on a Thursday for more strength

Connecting with Fog through Nature and Deity

Fog plays a critical role in nature – especially in coastal and mountainous regions such as the coastal redwood forests – and here below are a few ways how.

- 'Fog drip' is the term used for hydration that comes from fog. Trees and plants catch the fog drip, which drops to the ground and provides much-needed moisture
- Some plants absorb moisture directly from the fog itself, and this is known as 'foliar uptake'
- Fog supports biodiversity, particularly in hot regions, giving a moisture lifeline to rare plants
- Some animals in arid regions rely on fog as a source of moisture
- Fog can reduce water loss when it cloaks an area due to lowering the temperature by blocking the sun. Some animals also rely on fog for cooling their environment
- Through its deposited moisture, fog can provide nutrients for the soil
- Fog removes pollutants from the air by providing air filtration, known as 'wet scavenging'

There are many positive benefits that fog brings to nature; however, there are negative impacts also. Migrating birds can become lost due to fog, and it is this negative and hidden side we see in mythology and legends surrounding fog.

In Greek and Roman mythology, fog appears as a primordial mist or 'death mist', and in Celtic lore, the

Tuatha Dé Danann used a magical mist known as the *Féth Fiada* to make themselves invisible. In Italian folklore, fog was something to be avoided for fear of being attacked by a witch called *Borda*, who used the fog to hide in.

The closest we get to a fog deity is from Latvian mythology, where a group of mother goddesses called *Măte* are mentioned. They were thought to be distinct mother goddesses who were overseers of various aspects of life and nature. *Miglas Măte* was 'Mother of Fogs'.

Connecting with Storms and Fogs in Other Ways

- Make your own fog; details can be found online
- Make or buy a 'foggy', which is a type of pasty with a luxury filling
- Listen to the sounds of a storm
- Read or write a poem about storms or fog

FACELESS FOG

"It shrouds the mountains,
Smoky tendrils weave.
Smothering with grey,
Everything that breathes.
Its shapeshifting form,
Creeps in every space.
A mysterious presence,
Without a face."

CHAPTER SIX

White and Bright – Snow and Auroras

Snow

Snow is made up of individual ice crystals that grow in the atmosphere, usually in clouds, then fall and accumulate on the ground, creating a winter's landscape that captures beauty and peace. Many of us like the idea of the perfect snowy scene but tend not to like the melting stage when the snow turns to slush and becomes dirty. Slush and snowmelt, however, are good for releasing.

Connecting with Snow Spiritually and Magically

Snow symbolises many things, such as peace, purity, and transformation. As it is magically connected to the element of water, it can be used in workings for emotions, cleansing, relationships, love, and purification. Snow is also connected in a small part to the elements of earth and air, through the way it forms and how it falls.

After a heavy snowfall, have you ever noticed how quiet the world becomes? This is the perfect time to go out to really appreciate the wonder and beauty of snow.

Snow Stillness

After a heavy snowfall, go out early before people start to rise. Ideally, find a spot in nature and make sure you dress appropriately. When you have arrived at a quiet spot, just stand and look all around you. Feel the atmosphere; notice the silence, the peace. Watch how the winter sun glints upon the snow. Let the almost monochrome beauty and tranquillity wash over you. When you feel ready, and before you get too cold, head home.

Snow Transformation

Snow is a wonderful medium to mould into shapes to use for change. The simplest way is to make a small snow figure to represent yourself. As you are making it, think of something you would like to change for the better in yourself. Focus on this and send this intention into your snow figure. You could say a few words.

> "Snow of transformation, make a change in me, shape me in a better way, one of positivity."

Let your snow figure melt and transform, releasing your positive intention out into the world.

Snowfall Visualisation

Here in Britain, not every region will have a snowfall, never mind a significant one, but the magic of snow can still be worked with through visualisation. Here is an example of one but it's always great to write your own.

Find somewhere quiet where you will not be disturbed and get comfortable in a seated position, with your back straight but not rigid. Gently close your eyes or turn your focus to one object and take a few calming breaths. Let us begin.

The day is turning to dusk, and silently from the sky a single snowflake falls. Fluttering through the sky, it lands on the palm of your hand. One tiny, intricate, unique, and beautiful flake.

(Pause)

As it begins to melt in the warmth of your hand, more snowflakes start falling from the sky. Only a few at first, but soon more join the merry dance, waltzing in fading light, capturing the silence as they fall.

(Pause)

The moon rises, gleaming bright, and the snow continues falling, sparkling in the silvery glow of the lunar light. You watch, mesmerised, embracing the tranquillity of the moment.

(Pause)

Down the snowflakes tumble in the quiet of night; joining together, they lie on the ground in harmony, creating a carpet of glittering white.

(Pause)

A hush descends on the land. Stay a while, watch a while, allow the silence to bring you peace.

When you feel ready, slowly open your eyes or bring your focus back. Have a drink and a nibble on some food. Write down any thoughts.

Auroras

Yes, auroras are weather. They are not what one would consider as traditional weather; however, they are classed as 'space weather'.

They occur when solar wind collides with the earth's magnetic field, causing a geomagnetic storm, the visible manifestation of which is the aurora, which scientists often refer to as 'the light show after the storm'.

The best place to see one is in the 'auroral band' that covers Finland, Sweden, Norway and Iceland, but it can be seen even here in Britain in the far north of Scotland with the right conditions of clear skies and no light pollution. The further south of Britain you are, the less likely you are to see one, but it is not impossible, and auroras have been seen further south, even in recent years.

Connecting with Auroras Spiritually and Magically

Auroras are a fantastic light show to be utterly mesmerised by, and if you do get the opportunity to see one, then definitely do so and bathe in its gloriousness. They are connected to the element of fire, so can be used magically for banishing, cleansing, confidence, empowerment, joy, manifestation, purification, rebirth, strength, transformation, and vitality. The element of air also has a connection with auroras.

Joyful Heart

This can be done outside under an aurora, as a visualisation or when watching a video of auroras.

Focus on the lights, the shapes, the colours, and the movements. Utterly immerse yourself in the beauty, and say:

> "In darkest night, may your colours bright, fill me with your shining light,
> Chase the darkness from my heart, and fill me with your radiant spark."

Connecting with Snow through Science, History and Lore

Snow was described in a book in 135 BCE by Han Ying, where he contrasted the symmetry of flowers to the symmetry of snowflakes, and it was Albertus Magnus who provided the earliest European description in 1250. Extensive research came in 1932 when Ukichiro Nakaya began his studies by growing snowflakes and classified them into seven main types. This research has now been extended with many more different forms of snowflake and includes prisms, plates, columns, needles, and dendrites. It is the dendrites that give us our most beloved representation of the snowflake.

The word 'snow' comes from the Old English word *snaw*, but it is known and has been known by many different terms all over the world. In Scotland, there are 421 separate terms connected to snow, such as 'flindrikin', used to describe a slight snow shower, and 'blin-drift', which refers to thick drifting snow.

In the 19th century, we had the word 'greymin' for a meagre fall of snow, a 'hap' for a heavy blanketing, and a 'wap whap' to describe a sudden heavy snowstorm.

'Ninguid' was a term used in 1656 to describe all covered in snow, and 'frost dogs' were tiny frozen particles of falling snow. A single flake of snow was referred to as a 'flother' in the 13th century and a 'snow blossom' in 1676. It was not until over 60 years later that the word 'snowflake' would come into being.

Snowfall comes in several types and is described as having varied conditions. The main types of snow include 'dry/powder snow', which is light and fluffy; 'graupel', which are snow pellets; and 'wet/heavy snow', which is the type that sticks together and is great for making snowmen.

The weather conditions of snow pertain to the intensity as to which the snow is falling.

Snow flurries – light and intermittent with little or no accumulation.

Snow shower – moderate in intensity but brief.

Snow squall – sudden and intense heavy snowfall, often accompanied by high winds but short-lived.

Snowfall – steady extended fall with accumulation.

Heavy snowfall – intense, extended with accumulation.

Blizzard – severe with winds over 35 mph, low visibility and lasts for at least three hours.

Snow comes under a different terminology once it is lying on the ground and other surfaces and includes terms such as 'powder', 'slush', 'corn snow', and 'crust'. Even today, as throughout history, there are many words to describe snow.

Crystalline Snowflakes

Something scientific to try is to create your own snow-like crystals.

You will need:

- A clean jam jar
- Epsom salts
- Hot water
- A spoon
- A fridge

Pour Epsom salts into the jar to ¾ full. Carefully add the hot water until the salts are covered. Stir well and keep stirring until all the salts have dissolved. It's ok to have a few grains still left in the bottom. Place the jar in the fridge, and after a few hours you will have a jar of snowflake-like crystals.

Carefully pour the water out to study – and as a cautionary note: Epsom salts should not be eaten!

Weather Lore

"A year of snow, a year of plenty."

This saying is rooted in old agriculture and refers to snowfall covering the ground through the entirety of winter, and while accurate, this is a rare occurrence in Britain today. The reason for its accuracy is due to the snow-covered ground; the growing process is delayed until after the frost snaps, which are liable to kill new plants. It also means the process of thawing and refreezing does not occur, which is good for wheat and grain.

Connecting with Auroras through Science, History and Lore

The earliest recorded aurora is from Ancient China in 977 or 957 BCE, and Seneca wrote about auroras in his first book. Further auroras were recorded by Pytheas in the 4th century, and the most intense geomagnetic storm to be recorded was the Carrington Event of

1859. It peaked on the 1st and 2nd of September and created auroral displays that were seen globally. Elias Loomis published a series of papers on the event after he had collected worldwide reports.

It was in the 1900's that the first scientific explanation of auroras was published and credited to Kristian Birkeland, a Norwegian scientist, although it was Galileo who coined the term 'aurora borealis' in 1619. In modern times, auroras and geomagnetic storms are studied extensively with the topic of space weather, which also covers solar storms, solar winds, and solar flares.

The colours of the aurora are very much dependent on the gases present in the atmosphere and the altitude at which the solar particles collide.

Green – occurs at a lower altitude where oxygen is present and is the most common.

Red – occurs at high altitude where oxygen is present.

Pink and Purple – occurs at a lower altitude when nitrogen is present.

Blue – a less common occurrence that appears when nitrogen is present in the lower atmosphere.

Yellow – occurs when activity is intense and is accompanied by solar storms or solar flares.

You can work with the aurora's colours magically by matching the aurora's colour with its magical correspondence.

Green – prosperity, fertility, health, growth and good luck.

Red – energy, health, willpower, love and passion.

Pink – friendship, romance, emotional healing and harmony.

Purple – intuition, psychic ability, wisdom and power.

Blue – peace, calm, communication, and healing.

Yellow – intellect, creativity, happiness and friendship.

Create an Aurora

Another way to work with aurora colours is to create an aurora. Take different coloured glow sticks and place them into separate glasses of water. When dark, tap the glasses and watch the aurora colours radiate from them.

Cultural interpretations of auroras as signs vary, with Britain and France seeing them as a bad omen of things to come, including war, which was strengthened when in 1939 the aurora was visible as far south as London and seen as a herald to the Second World War.

In China, Japan and Australia, auroras are seen as being more favourable. China associates them with dragons, and in Japan it is thought that any child conceived under the Northern Lights would be blessed with good fortune.

Native American tribes hold the belief that the aurora is the spirits of the deceased but have varied views on what the spirits are doing.

In Iceland and Greenland, the lights are linked to birth, while in Sweden they were seen as a gift from the gods. In Finland, the northern lights are known as 'revontulet', which means 'firefox', and it was believed that the aurora was caused by sparks flying from the firefox's tail as it ran.

There is no specific weather lore on auroras, but they are seen more as an omen or a portent of future life events by some.

Connecting with Snow through Nature and Deity

- Snow is important for the planet, not least of all for the plants and animals of the tundra who rely on the snow for their survival due to their biological makeup, but in other parts of the world too, including here in Britain
- Snow insulates the soil, preventing it from freezing completely, which is good for the soil and those creatures living within the soil
- Snow captures nutrients from the atmosphere as it falls, which the soil benefits from, as small amounts of nitrogen are one of the nutrient elements captured
- Snow can suppress weeds and pests, giving gardeners and farmers a head start with their own crops
- Snow is needed by certain animals for camouflaging themselves from predators. The Arctic hare, for example, changes its coat from brown to white in the winter for this reason
- Snowmelt provides water for the soil and fills rivers and reservoirs, which is an essential process in some regions of the world

Considering how impactful snow can be upon nature and humans alike, there are very few deities associated with snow specifically, and those known have little written about them. Tengliu is a snow goddess from Chinese mythology, Chione is from the Greek pantheon, and Ullr is a god from the Norse pantheon.

Another snow figure is Asiaq, who comes from Inuit mythology, where she is known as a weather goddess or 'Mother of Weather'. She was the one responsible for deciding how much snow fell and when it fell. For those living in Greenland, she was an important figure, as she was the one who brought about the snowmelt which they relied upon. Spiritual leaders or shamans would go and speak to Asiaq to ask her for good weather.

Rather than work with a deity, when it comes to snow, I always think it is rather nice to appreciate snow as it is by creating an altar in honour of the weather condition.

Ideas for a Snow Altar

- White candles
- Snowflake-shaped objects
- White, silver, or pale blue colours
- Snowmelt water
- Snow pictures, art, or photos
- Animal ornaments connected to the snow
- Plants connected to the snow
- Snow quartz
- Snow globe

Connecting with Auroras through Nature and Deity

Auroras do impact nature, but not in a permanent or life-threatening way. In fact, the auroras themselves are a reassuring sign that the earth's magnetic field is protecting the planet from solar winds.

The way in which nature is affected is in the temporary disruption of magnetism. Some animals use the earth's magnetic cues to aid in their migration, and the aurora puts this off kilter for a short while, although, due to its non-permanence, the migrating animals do not get put off track too much. The light of the aurora also gives a false sense of daylight, affecting animals' natural nighttime, but again, this is temporary.

It is perhaps due to the temporariness of the aurora that led many of the ancient cultures to see the aurora as being divine but not really have a deity specifically named as being connected to it. The Chuvash people of Siberia did interpret the aurora as being a manifestation of their heaven god, who helped women in childbirth.

According to V.K. Magnitsky, the Northern Lights was a deity named Surlan, although scant evidence has been discovered, and there is much dispute as to whether this character was a god or a lesser spirit creator.

Although the aurora, and particularly the aurora borealis, is named after two deities, neither is connected to the phenomenon of the lights. Aurora is the goddess of the dawn, and Borealis is taken from the god of the north wind.

Spiritually, it is up to the individual to decide what the aurora stands for, and I like to think of it as being all the lost beautiful souls of the world.

Connecting with Snow and Auroras in Other Ways

SNOW

- Make a magical snowman poppet
- Collect snow and save it in the freezer for future workings
- Make a snowman
- Sledge, ski, or snowboard
- Throw snowballs
- Photograph snowy landscapes or snowflakes up close
- Listen to music that reminds you of snow; create a playlist
- Make paper snowflakes
- Make a snow globe
- Read or write a poem about snow

AMID THE FALLING SNOW

"Deep in the forest, where no one ever goes,
There comes a kind of hush amid the gently falling
snow.
The birds have gone to roost, all of nature starts to
slow,
The land slips into slumber, amid the gently falling
snow.

Naked trees they stand in reverence, as the silence starts to grow,
And the earth becomes at peace, amid the gently falling snow."

AURORAS

- Say a prayer for the souls of the deceased in the aurora
- Wave sparklers like the firefox's tail
- Create an aurora picture with chalks on black paper
- Read or write a poem about the aurora
- Watch the aurora set to relaxing music
- Hold a light party
- Follow the 'aurora tracker' online

CHAPTER SEVEN

Weird and Wonderful Weather

Weather is amazing! Every morning the sun rises; with the right conditions, it rains or snows – it is like a miracle every day. Even more amazing, however, are rare weather types and weather phenomena. Instances of it happen worldwide and vary anywhere from the weird to the wonderful.

Ball Lightning – A rare weather phenomenon, described as glowing, floating orbs during a thunderstorm. In the accounts recorded, the ball lightning varies in size but most commonly measures 10 to 20 cm in diameter and has been reported in a range of colours, including red, orange, white, yellow and blue. Most observer accounts said that there was no heat from the ball, but there was an odour of burning sulphur.

One of the earliest written references to ball lightning is from an English monk, dated 1195, where he describes a fiery globe coming from a cloud and falling towards the river. Another account from 1638 tells of how a ball of fire entered the church and then split into two before disappearing after causing much damage.

Though much scientific research has been undertaken, ball lightning still remains a mystery.

Black Blizzards – These were severe dust storms that occurred in the 1930's across the Great Plains of America. They occurred due to a very dry season and soil being whipped up by winds that looked black from the dirt. Visibility was almost zero, and the event caused devastation and left people with dust pneumonia.

Black Ice – Despite its name, black ice is a thin and almost transparent layer of ice and one of winter's deadliest hazards, due to it having no traction and being hard to see. It occurs when water or humidity meets an already below-freezing ground surface.

Blood Rain – This phenomenon has been recorded since the 8th century, when it was initially thought to be blood falling from the sky and considered a bad omen. There have been many cases of blood rain throughout history, including one from Southern England in 1968. The cause is due to sand, dust, and/

or microorganisms being carried in the atmosphere and then falling with the rain.

Diamond Dust – Only seen on extremely cold days, and a rare occurrence in Britain, it is where the water vapour in the air turns into tiny ice crystals which glitter like diamonds when the sun's light catches them.

Dust Devil – This is a small and short-lived whirlwind of energy that picks up things in its path as it travels, such as dirt, hay, or any other light debris. It usually occurs on a summer's day when the heat is intense yet the air above is quite cool.

Fall Streak – This is when a hole appears in a bank of clouds and almost resembles a rift in space and time.

Fire Devils – Also known as 'fire whirls', these take place during forest fires or wildfires and are vortexes of flame which rotate vertically, sometimes reaching up to a height of 300 metres.

Fire Rainbow – A rare optical phenomenon formed by the refraction of sunlight through ice crystals in high-altitude cirrus clouds, it displays as a horizontal rainbow that resembles the flames of a fire.

Fogbow – A rainbow that appears as a ghostly arc of white light appearing out of the backdrop of fog. It is caused by the refraction, reflection, and diffraction of light in water droplets, which erases the colour spectrum.

Frost Quake – Usually occurring at night, a frost quake happens when a sudden extreme drop in temperature freezes the water in the ground. This creates tension, and on expansion and release of the ground fracturing, there is a loud noise and an exceptionally light tremor.

Glory – This is an optical effect where a rainbow halo appears around the shadow of a person and usually happens in high areas such as mountains. It is caused by sunlight interacting with tiny water droplets and is sometimes thought to be a concentric rainbow. A concentric rainbow, however, is much larger than a glory and does not focus around a point.

In China, a glory is known as 'Buddha's Light' and is often observed on the cloud-cloaked Mount Emei, with records of sightings here going back to 63 CE.

Heat Burst – These can occur in the wake of a dying storm where the conditions are right, and when a heat burst comes from the atmosphere in one sudden burst, raising the temperature in an area briefly but by a significant amount.

Heatwave – The heatwave of 2003 was so hot that the grapes on the vines were turned to raisins.

Ice Discs – Also known as 'ice circles' and 'ice pancakes', this rare natural phenomenon occurs in slow-moving water. It is where thin circular slabs of ice form on the water and slowly rotate on the surface. They vary in size but can reach over 15 metres in diameter. They are created through vortexes of water capturing a piece of ice which is spun and ground to form a perfect disc shape.

Ice discs have been seen in many locations, and the Presumpscot River in Westbrook, Maine, has seen recurring ice discs in many years, but they have been reported in other places, such as Wales in 2008 and England in 2009. They are most frequently seen in North America and Scandinavia.

Light Pillars – These are long streaks of multi-coloured light beaming from the sky. They require specific conditions to occur, including freezing to sub-zero temperatures and calm, windless nights. They are caused by tiny ice crystals hanging in the atmosphere reflecting an available source of light, which could be the sun, the moon or even streetlights.

Night Sprites – Also known as 'red sprites', these have been reported since 1886 and are large-scale electrical discharges that occur far above an active thunderstorm, usually triggered by strong cloud-to-ground lightning strikes. Lasting for milliseconds, they can reach 30 miles high and form in clusters that have been likened to a carrot shape.

Roll Cloud – Classed as a 'volutus cloud' in the *International Cloud Atlas*, this is a long, horizontal, low-level dark cloud that looks like the crest of a large wave as it is breaking. Mostly, but not exclusively seen at the coast, they are created by wind shear and can last for several hours and extend for miles. In 2025, on the coast of Portugal, witnesses of a roll cloud described it as looking like a tsunami.

Snow Roller – This extremely rare phenomenon needs the perfect conditions of moisture, snow, wind, and temperature to occur and appears as a doughnut-like formation of rolled snow. They are usually seen in hilly areas, and examples have been found in Germany, Poland, the USA, and even in England in 2019.

St. Elmo's Fire – Known by many other names, this is a weather phenomenon where luminous plasma is released when the air molecules around an object are ionised, giving off a blue or violet glow, often accompanied by a hissing or buzzing noise.

Named after St. Erasmus of Formia, the patron saint of sailors, the phenomenon was regarded well by sailors, as it could be a warning of a lightning strike.

It has been sighted since ancient times and is referenced in accounts of historical notables such as Julius Caesar, Pliny the Elder, William Bligh, Charles Darwin, and Nikola Tesla, who created St. Elmo's fire in 1899 when testing a Tesla coil. It has been known by many names over time, including 'Helene' by the Ancient Greeks and *'canwyll yr ysbryd'* by Welsh seamen, which means 'candles of the Holy Ghost', and the Russian mariners referred to it as St. Peter's Lights.

Strange Rains – This is a rare phenomenon where something other than rain is falling from the sky and usually consists of flightless animals. Incidents have been reported in many places throughout the world, with the most common fall being that of fish, but others include frogs, worms, jellyfish, and even meat.

The Kentucky Meat Shower was one of the strangest examples, occurring in 1876, where chunks of red meat fell from the sky in a 90 by 45 metre area over several minutes. The exact cause remains a mystery, though many theories have been put forward, including vultures, which will vomit when making a quick escape as a defensive measure.

As for animal rain, the earliest references are in the Bible as one of the ten plagues of Egypt, and Athenaeus talks about a rain of fish in 4th-century Greece. Other occurrences throughout history include a rain of frogs in Belgium in 1625, toads in France in 1794, worms in Memphis in 1877, and even jellyfish in England in 1894.

One of the first scientists to take accounts and provide a theory regarding animal rain was André-Marie Ampère (1775–1836). He suggested that violent winds were picking up the animals from one place and depositing them somewhere else.

More recent reports have been of tiny pink frogs in England in 1987, fish in Wales in 2004, and marine animals in China in 2018. In Yoro, Honduras, fish have rained on the city every year for a century, usually between May and July, and this is known as 'Lluvia de Peces'.

Virga – A phenomenon of ghostly precipitation that never makes it to the ground due to it evaporating before it gets to the earth's surface, yet leaving feathery streaks extending from the base of the cloud. It is caused by the air beneath the cloud being very dry.

Watermelon Snow – Also known as 'red snow', 'pink snow' and 'blood snow', this is where the snow is reddish in colour, and it is caused by a species of algae called *Chlamydomonas nivalis*, which thrives in cold conditions. It is common in coastal polar areas and alpine regions.

Watermelon snow was first recorded in Aristotle's writings and puzzled naturalists for many years. It was in 1818 that Robert Brown, a Scottish botanist and palaeobotanist, after a voyage where they witnessed red snow, tentatively theorised that it was caused by algae.

However, watermelon snow isn't the only colour that snow has been reported as being, and other colours include blue, green, orange and yellow.

Weather Extremes from Around the World

The earth's temperature ranges wildly, with the hottest recorded at 56°C in the USA, and the lowest at -89°C in Antarctica. A few other extremes include:

- The largest hailstone on record is 47.3 cm in diameter
- The longest lightning bolt to date is measured at 515 miles
- The most tornadoes in one day stands at 207 and occurred in the USA
- The most snow in one day fell on the village of Capracotta in Italy in 2015 and was 256 cm deep

Britain's Unbelievable Weather Extremes

- The highest temperature recorded in Britain is 40.3°C in 2022, and the lowest stands at -27.2°C in 1982
- The deepest snowfall occurred on 14th March 1947 and was 211 cm deep
- November 23rd in 1981 is recorded as having the most tornadoes in Britain, with a total of 104 making touchdown
- On June 2nd in 1975 it snowed, causing cricket matches to be abandoned. While this was a rare occurrence, it wasn't a first, and previous snow in June had been recorded in 1888

CHAPTER EIGHT

The Weather Lore Year

An interesting way of connecting with the weather throughout the year is through weather lore, observation and associations. You can go as in-depth with it as you wish or just pick out a few weather lore dates to observe. For either activity, you will need somewhere to record your findings.

Weather lore is a collection of informal knowledge related to or predicting the weather. Much of it is from the old agricultural way of life, passed down through the spoken and written word – the observations of nature and the weather by everyday people, in contrast to the scientific methods used today.

There are hundreds of weather lore sayings, with some often being similar to each other and only varying slightly due to regional dialects and culture. An example of this is:

"Red sky at night, shepherds delight" and *"Red sky at night, sailors delight."*

Every month had weather lore attached to it, and often the Christian feast days held a weather prediction of some kind.

Much weather lore still stands as being fairly reliable even today; perhaps you could keep a weather lore journal to observe how many of the following examples for the year are still relevant in current times.

January

- *"A January spring is worth nothing"*
- *"January blossoms fill no man's cellar"*
- 12th – St. Bernard – *"If the sun shines, it foreshows much wind"*
- 13th – St. Hilary – *"Supposed to be the coldest day of the year"*
- 22nd – St. Vincent – *"If on this day the sky is clear, more wine than water will crown the year"*
- 25th – St. Paul – *"If the sun shines, it betokens a good year. If rain or snow, indifferent. If misty, it predicts great dearth. If thunder, great winds and death of people"*

An alternative saying for today, as it is also St. Ananias' Day, states:

"If St. Ananias be fair and clear, it betokened a happy year,
But if it chance to snow or rain, dear will be all sorts of grain.
If clouds or mist do dark the sky, great store of birds and beasts will die,
And if the winds do fly a lot, then wars shall vex the kingdom oft."

February

- *If the cat lies in the sun in February, she will creep behind the stove in March*
- *If it thunders in February, it will frost in April*
- 2nd – Candlemas, St. Brigid, Groundhog Day – A few weather lore indicators belong to this day including:

  "If this day be fair and bright, winter puts up another fight.
  If this day be dull and grey, winter's gone and won't come again."

In the US and Canada, some still celebrate Groundhog Day as a weather prediction to see if winter is over, and in Europe there is a similar prediction – observing a badger instead of a groundhog. Weather lore from Germany states that:

"If the badger is in the sun at Candlemas, he will have to go back into his hole for another four weeks."

March

- "March winds and April showers bring forth May flowers"
- "As many mists in March as there are frosts in May"
- "As it rains in March, so it rains in June"

April

- *"If early April is foggy, rain in June will make lanes boggy"*
- *"When April blows its horn, 'tis good for hay and corn"* (blowing its horn refers to it being windy)

May

- "A cold May is kindly and fills the barn finely"
- "A swarm of bees in May is worth a load of hay"
- "Mist in May, heat in June, makes the harvest come right soon"

June

- *"If June is sunny, harvest comes early"*
- *"A cold wet June pools the rest of the year"*
- 8th – St. Medard – *"If it rains today, it foretells a wet harvest"*
- 11th – St. Barnabas – *"Always fine weather today"*
- 29th – St. Peter and Paul – *"Rain today will rot the roots of the rye"*

July

- *"A shower of rain in July, when the corn begins to fill, is worth a plough of oxen, and all belongs there till"*
- 15th – St. Swithun – *"If on this day it rains, for forty days it will remain"*

August

- "Dry August and warm, does harvest no harm"
- "August rain gives honey, wine and saffron"
- "If the first week of August is warm, the winter will be white and long"
- 24th – St. Bartholomew – *"If it be fair and clear, a prosperous autumn comes that year"*

September

- 29th – Michaelmas – St. Michael – *"A dark day today means a light Christmas"*

October

- *"Rain in October means wind in December"*
- *"If October moon comes without a frost, expect no frost 'til the moon of November"*
- 31st – Hallowtide – *"If ducks slide at Hallowtide, by Christmas they will swim. If ducks swim at Hallowtide, by Christmas they will slide"*

November

- *"Thunder in November means winter will be late in coming and going"*
- *"A warm November is a sign of bad weather"*
- 1st – All Saints Day – *"If the weather is clear, 'tis the end of the sowing year"*
- 11th – Martinmas – St. Martin – *"Wind in the northwest, there's a severe winter on the way. Wind in the southwest, there it will remain 'til February, and a mild winter will come to play"*
- 23rd – St. Clement – *"This day brings the winter"*

- 25th – St. Catherine – *"If today is foul or fair, so will be next February"*

December

- *"Thunder in December presages fine weather"*
- *"A green Christmas makes a fat churchyard"*
- 21st – St. Thomas – There are two weather lore sayings for today; the first states: *"If it freezes today, then the price of corn will fall, and if it's mild, the price of corn will rise,"* and the second states: *"Look at the weathercock on St. Thomas' Day at 12 o'clock and see which way the wind is, for there it will stick for the next lunar quarter"*
- 25th – Christmas Day – *"If the sun shines through the apple tree on Christmas Day, there will be an abundant crop in the following year"*
- 31st – New Year's Eve –

> "If New Year's Eve the wind blows south,
> It betokened warmth and growth.
> If west, much milk and fish in the sea,
> If north, cold and storms there will be.
> If east, the trees will bear much fruit,
> If northeast, then flee it man and brute (beast)"

Observation

Observations of the weather can be recorded in many ways, from as simple as just noting down whether it was cloudy, sunny, or rainy, to including other aspects and conditions. For example, one year I included data from my barometer, another year I recorded temperatures, and one year I included what was happening in nature. Plants and animals can often be a good indicator of weather, as they seem to be more in tune with the natural world than humans often are.

When did the first flowers bloom, when did you see the first bee or butterfly, when did you spot the first brood of ducklings, or when did the geese or other migratory birds reappear? You could also record any unusual weather, which is always fascinating to look back at in years to come. Of course, you do not have to go as in-depth as this, but it is an interesting activity, and if you wanted to go further in-depth, then you could look at measuring rainfall, snowfall, or wind speeds.

If you do want to go more in-depth, there are a few tools you may find useful.

- A journal of some kind to record everything in
- Your phone camera is an ideal way to record weather or nature happenings, as the photo has a date stamp
- A weathervane to show which direction the wind is blowing
- A rain gauge to measure rainfall – simple ones can be made at home using a plastic bottle, or they can be bought quite cheaply
- A ruler to measure snowfall
- A thermometer to record the temperature
- An anemometer, which measures the speed of the wind. This too can be made simply at home, and speed is measured by counting the rotations in a 60-second period. There are tutorials online

- A barometer, which measures air pressure and gives a barometric reading as to what the weather is. Analogue barometers have a hand rather like a clock which moves to indicate the pressure in millimetres and millibars. The lower readings foretell rain, mid-range as changeable, and high readings as fair weather. Nowadays there are digital barometers which give all the weather details on their display and are easy to take the data from

Here are a few excerpts from my weather observations in 2018:

February 27th – It is a strange snow today, like tiny polystyrene balls falling from the skies and littering the ground.

April 14th – Finally, the pink blossom has started appearing!

May 9th – Bluebells have bloomed in abundance now, spilling their colour under a canopy of green leaves. All of a sudden, nature has burst forth, singing its song for all to hear and see.

September 15th – First conker (horse chestnut).

September 23rd – It is still. The odd bird calls through the gloom, but besides that mournful lament, it is eerily quiet in the grey drizzle. There is a bit of a chill this morning, the type of chill that seeps into your being. Paths are littered with torn debris from the last three days of winds wild and shrieking, and it is the first day that I have felt I needed gloves.

September 29th – The day has dawned bright, but the sun has lost its fervent heat; it can no longer penetrate the icy cold of the still air.

October 6th – Nature looks rather sad and bedraggled this morning, the leaves on the ground turning to sodden mush from the stream of unrelenting rain throughout the night.

October 10th – It is a beautifully warm afternoon with skies of pale blue. If it were not for the saffron-coloured leaves shining as they fall, you could be mistaken that it was spring. The ladybirds are out, multitudes of scarlet and black, flying in the heat of the autumn sunshine.

October 16th – A thick fog cloaks the landscape this morning. The first fog this season.

October 27th – The first frost lies on the ground this morning.

November 3rd – We have ladybirds in the shed. Quite a veritable little group huddled together, keeping warm against the ever-invading chill of winter. The nights and mornings are very cold now, with Jack Frost making a brief appearance for the last few days. He seems half-hearted in his frosty efforts, or maybe it's a little taste of what is to come.

November 5th – Grey, misty with mizzle in the air. The sun is there; I occasionally catch a tiny glimpse of it through small breaks in the cloud.

November 17th – Wintery and cold.

November 21st – Snow was forecast last night, but none materialised; a shame, the conditions had seemed so right, and there's nothing like a sprinkling of snow to brighten winter's grey.

November 24th – Grey, damp, and cold.

From these snippets, you can build up a picture of the weather and gain a closer and deeper connection to the weather and nature. When you keep a weather journal for a few years in a row, it is interesting to compare how the weather varied or see if any patterns emerged.

Your weather observation could take other forms. I write nature poetry, where I often include the weather conditions, but a photographic record would work well, or an artist's account; it could even just be seasonal observations.

Observing the weather is worthwhile for connecting, not just in a practical way, but also spiritually and magically too. It allows us to appreciate the miracle that weather is and how each weather type can help us or be used for well-being and magical workings.

Magical Associations

By observing weather, we learn how we can magically connect with it and how it can help us. Noticing which elements the weather is associated with, what colour is relevant, and its personality or shape all help to determine what magical workings would work best.

For example, if you wished to work with the clouds on an overcast day, the elements would be air and water, as these are the building blocks that make up a cloud. But what colour are the clouds? What shapes are they? Are they low in the sky? All these factors can be looked at – and also use your intuition. If you get a feeling that these clouds are good for communication, then go with it.

As a guide, here are the general magical associations:

Elements

Fire – banishing, cleansing, confidence, empowerment, joy, manifestation, purification, rebirth, strength, transformation, and vitality.

Air – cleansing, communication, divination, focus, and visualisation.

Water – emotions, cleansing, love, scrying, relationships, intuition, and purification.

Earth – abundance, career, fertility, grounding, growth, healing, luck, nourishment, peace, prosperity, protection, stillness, and wisdom.

Colours

Red – love, energy, health, and willpower.

Orange – change, encouragement, and power.

Yellow – intellect, creativity, happiness, and friendship.

Green – prosperity, fertility, health, growth, and good luck.

Blue – healing, calm, communication, and peace.

Violet/Purple – divination, nurturing, wisdom, and balance.

White – cleansing, clarity, and order.

Black – banishing, releasing negativity, and transformation.

Brown – balance, concentration, and home.

Grey – decisions, binding negativity, and compromise.

Indigo – meditation, spiritual healing, and clarity of purpose.

Pink – emotional healing, romance, harmony, and friendship.

Silver – spiritual development, meditation, and warding off negativity.

Gold – success, health, ambition, finances, and fortune.

Numbers

1 – self-reliance and personal ability.

2 – partnership and peace.

3 – growth, fertility, creativity, and luck.

4 – practical matters and stability.

5 – communication and movement.

6 – home, love, and pleasure.

7 – spirituality and guidance.

8 – intensity and extremity.

9 – compassion and helping others.

10 – completion and unity.

Seasonal Associations

Weather itself changes with the seasons; rain in spring feels different to rain in winter, as does the sunshine. Because of this, seasonal associations can be worked within your weather magic.

Spring – renewal, fertility, new beginnings, youth, awakening, and growth.

Summer – passion, strength, energy, joy, light, and abundance.

Autumn – harvest, balance, reflection, change, letting go, and maturity.

Winter – rest, reflection, death and rebirth, silence, and inner work.

The Weather Oracle

Another way I like to work with the weather is as an oracle or in contemplation. Over the years of connecting with weather, I have intuitively associated them with key words and created my own cards that I work with. I will pull one card from the deck and either contemplate on the word or use that word as my focus for the day. This is an activity you could do yourself; you do not have to be a brilliant artist. Just visualise a weather condition, and using your intuition, record what word comes to mind. Then draw the weather condition on a card and write the word that you associated with it.

As an example, here are a few of my own:

Blazing Sunshine – Strength.

Sunshine/Cloud – Balance.

Heavy Rain – Self-care.

Gentle Breeze – Memories.

Spring Gusts – Renewal.

Autumn Gales – Release.

Thunderstorm – Power.

Summer Rain – Joy.

Gently Falling Snow – Peace.

I hope I have given you some insight into working with the weather in magical, spiritual and practical ways. It really is an amazing part of nature, and by connecting with it, mind, body and soul, we can enhance our lives and appreciate the miracle that weather really is, even on the gloomy days.

References

BOOKS

Valerie Porter: *The Little Book of Weatherlore* (2011).
Zoe Johnson: *The Weather Almanac* (2025).
David Pickering: *Cassell's Dictionary of Superstitions* (2002).
Paul Anthony Jones: *A Winter Dictionary* (2024).

MAGAZINES

Eco Kids Planet Magazine: Issue #135 (January, 2026).

WEBSITES

ahundredyearsago.com
metoffice.gov.uk
wiccaliving.com
countrylife.co.uk
thefield.co.uk
countryfile.com
bbc.co.uk

theaurorazone.com
cloudappreciationsociety.org
almanac.com
bbcearth.com
wikipedia.org
bloomineasyplants.com
bakerross.co.uk
snowcrystals.com
weather.gov
bgs.ac.uk
aurorareach.com
theoi.com

About the Author

Hannah Semple is a writer, poet, and blogger, with diplomas in naturopathy, colour therapy, and herbalism. She lives in South Wales with her partner and children, near to the Monmouthshire and Brecon Canal, which she finds a constant inspiration. You can find more of her writing at: www. earthmothernaturelover.wordpress.com

www.ingramcontent.com/pod-product-compliance
Ingram Content Group UK Ltd.
Pitfield, Milton Keynes, MK11 3LW, UK
UKHW021107190526
471172UK00001B/8